# Helping Kids and Teens with ADHD in School

*of related interest*

**ADHD – Living without Brakes**
*Martin L. Kutscher, M.D.*
*Illustrated by Douglas Puder, M.D.*
ISBN 978 1 84310 873 3

**All Dogs have ADHD**
*Kathy Hoopmann*
ISBN 978 1 84310 651 7

**Help Your Child or Teen Get Back on Track**
**What Parents and Professionals Can Do for Childhood Emotional and Behavioral Problems**
*Kenneth H. Talan, M.D.*
ISBN 978 1 84310 870 2

**Kids in the Syndrome Mix of ADHD, LD, Asperger's, Tourette's, Bipolar, and More!**
**The one stop guide for parents, teachers, and other professionals**
*Martin L. Kutscher MD*
*With a contribution from Tony Attwood*
*With a contribution from Robert R. Wolff MD*
ISBN 978 1 84310 810 8 (hb)
ISBN 978 1 84310 811 5 (pb)

**Cool Connections with Cognitive Behavioural Therapy**
**Encouraging Self-esteem, Resilience and Well-being in Children and Young People Using CBT Approaches**
*Laurie Seiler*
ISBN 978 1 84310 618 0

**Promoting Resilience in the Classroom**
**A Guide to Developing Pupils' Emotional and Cognitive Skills**
*Carmel Cefai*
*Foreword by Paul Cooper*
ISBN 978 1 84310 565 7

**Nature Groups in School and at Home**
**Connecting with Children with Social, Emotional and Behavioural Difficulties**
*Paul Cooper and Yonca Tiknaz*
ISBN 978 1 84310 528 2

**Helping Children to Build Self-Esteem**
**A Photocopiable Activities Book**
2nd edition
*Deborah M. Plummer*
*Illustrated by Alice Harper*
ISBN 978 1 84310 488 9

# Helping Kids and Teens with ADHD in School

A Workbook for Classroom Support and Managing Transitions

## Joanne Steer and Kate Horstmann

### Illustrated by Jason Edwards

Jessica Kingsley Publishers
London and Philadelphia

First published in 2009
by Jessica Kingsley Publishers
116 Pentonville Road
London N1 9JB, UK
and
400 Market Street, Suite 400
Philadelphia, PA 19106, USA

*www.jkp.com*

Copyright © Joanne Steer and Kate Horstmann 2009

Library of Congress Cataloging in Publication Data
A CIP catalog record for this book is available from the Library of Congress

British Library Cataloguing in Publication Data
A CIP catalogue record for this book is available from the British Library

ISBN 978 1 84310 663 0

Printed and bound in Great Britain by
MPG Books Group, Cornwall

# Contents

# Acknowledgements

**From Kate and Jo**: First, thanks to the wonderful team at the Croydon ADHD Network in South London. This cross-agency team, and the committed professionals within it, gave us the opportunity to work together and work creatively in response to the needs of young people and their families. In addition, we would like to thank our supportive base teams of that time – the Croydon Child and Adolescent Mental Health Service and the Croydon Children's Occupational Therapy Service (Croydon PCT). The biggest thanks however must go to all the young people and the families that we worked with, for their inspiration, perseverance and for teaching us so much. In particular, thanks to those members of the summer 'Transition' groups. We wish each of you all the best with your journeys!

**From Kate**: Thanks to my family and friends for their patience and support, and to Mum for her thorough editing and honest feedback. Thanks to all the inspirational professionals that I have worked with over the past ten years. In particular, thanks to Stephen Cleverdon and Alison Markwell, for offering me exceptional support and clinical freedom. Credit must go to my co-author, Jo, for thinking that we could not only write a book, but also have it published. Despite international relocations and a distance of around 14,000 kilometres, a wedding, a pregnancy, full-time work and demanding social calendars we made it!

**From Jo**: I would like to thank my husband James for his encouragement and support during the writing of this book. A special mention should also go to my baby – we are yet to meet, but you have been an amazing part of this journey. Thank you also goes to my Mum and to Claire Connolly for their advice and editing of previous versions – your comments were invaluable. The biggest thank you must go to Kate for agreeing to join me on this expedition of authorship and for being a fantastic co-author.

CHAPTER 1

# Welcome:
# An Introduction for Adults

Hello and welcome to our workbook! First, we are very excited that you have picked up this book and have at least read this much. We feel passionately about helping kids and teens with Attention Deficit Hyperactivity Disorder (ADHD) and Attention Deficit Disorder (ADD) and believe that sharing information, knowledge and strategies is the key to making a real difference in the lives and future of these young people. The ideas in this book have emerged from our work as clinicians in supporting young people with ADHD/ADD, their families and their schools. As a clinical psychologist (Jo) and occupational therapist (Kate), we have seen first hand the huge potential within these young people and the great outcomes that can be realized in working to support them. However, we have also seen the serious challenges often posed by a lack of understanding, support and resources.

We would anticipate that this book is most suited for use with children between the ages of 10 and 14 years. It is designed with a broad range of individuals in mind, including educators, teaching support staff, therapists, psychologists, ADHD coaches and parents. This book has a specific application in supporting the **transition to high school/secondary school**, and actually evolved from a group programme we developed to assist this process. For young people with a diagnosis of ADHD/ADD, and in particular for their families and school staff, this change is frequently a time of significant stress. The topics and activities covered in this book are felt to be important elements of the broad skill base required for coping effectively in high school. Key issues include managing stress, homework and friendships, and promoting concentration, organization and self-esteem. Therefore, only some of the worksheets and tip sheets are labelled as specifically addressing the 'mechanics' of transition. It follows that **young people already at high school** will also benefit from this book. While it is ideal for support and skill development to be provided in preparation for transition, these same strategies can be used effectively at any stage of their education! In fact it is ideal that the learning from this book is supported and extended well into a young person's high school career.

The underlying principles, from which this book is written, are the following:

1.  Acknowledging the individuality of young people with ADHD, and promoting their development of positive self-worth, underpins their success in achieving independence.

2.  Building relationships is vital – these young people can easily feel isolated and experience few positive and trusting relationships.

3.  Recognizing and understanding a problem is one of the biggest steps in making a real difference.

4. Knowledge and understanding needs to be shared with the young person in a way that makes sense to them, thus giving them the ownership and insight required for change.

5. Young people need to be involved in all steps of the process (learning, implementing and evaluating) in order to ensure that lasting change can be made.

6. Small changes can make a HUGE difference in the lives of these young people – choose only a few strategies at a time and do them well.

7. Strategies are only effective if they are tailored to the individual, introduced in a way that is consistent, and then evaluated and tweaked.

8. To work towards real independence, skills and coping techniques need to be taught in a planned and gradual manner with tangible assistance and support.

9. Adults need to meet the young person half way by making changes to their own behaviours as well as the surrounding environments and the nature of the tasks at hand.

10. Having FUN is essential when engaging and motivating young people with ADHD!

It is important to acknowledge that this book is not driven by specific research or theoretical approaches. It utilizes strategies from a variety of fields, and draws heavily on our clinical experience. For simplicity, the abbreviation ADHD is used to refer to all types of attention disorders. The strategies included have been carefully selected to ensure that they are all applicable in supporting the various forms of ADHD or ADD. We have chosen to *not* focus on issues such as prevalence, diagnosis and treatment, as there are many excellent resources available covering these topics. Some of the very basics of ADHD are dealt with in both this and the next chapter ('Getting Started') in a way that both young people and adults can access. However, we highly recommend actively following up some of the excellent resources listed throughout the book. We truly believe that understanding is the key!

We use three characters throughout the book to help young people to engage with the material: Carly, James and Zac. There are photocopiable images of each at the back of the book if you would like to create small posters and put them on the wall.

## HOW TO USE THIS BOOK

There are nine chapters (including this one) and each is divided into sections that should help you to navigate and plan. Each page and worksheet is labelled as one of the following:

#  Introducing

**Key purpose**: These pages provide insights and perspectives on the relevant topic and how it relates to young people with ADHD and the challenges of high school. They are designed more for adults than young people, though you'll notice that this section in Chapter 2 is written as an introduction for the young person, and is designed to be read with an adult. 'Introducing' sections also provide outlines as to the broad objectives for each chapter.

**User tips**: Read through this section before starting work on a chapter, so that you can plan how to discuss and explore the topic with the young person. The objectives/goals provided can be included in any support plans that may need to be developed around your work (e.g. Education Support Plans).

#  Detect and Reflect

**Key purpose**: 'Detect and Reflect' worksheets encourage the young person to think about the topic, their individual skills in this area and how other people around them think about this issue. 'Detect and Reflect' also attempts to broaden perspectives on issues in order to help normalize experiences, and lays the foundation for problem solving and goal setting.

**User tips**: The worksheets have been ordered in a way that is intended to build on a concept, but you can 'cut and paste' them as you see fit. Discussions around these do not always have to occur while sitting at a table – you can have them while kicking a ball around! Sometimes adding extra examples can help facilitate reflection and consideration, and help to broaden the young person's perspectives. These can be shared in an indirect way such as: 'Another person I know does... Is that something that happens to you?' It is ideal to come back to these worksheets and add in details that you might think of at other times (e.g. when doing the activities from the book).

#  Give It A Go

**Key purpose**: 'Give It A Go' worksheets ask the young person to trial a range of strategies as well as solve problems. There is often an added element of evaluating and rating the effectiveness of strategies and their potential for use in daily life.

**User tips**: Some of these tasks demand more preparation and completion time than others so forward planning is required. Most tasks don't need to be completed in the set order; however, it is always good to have done the 'Detect and Reflect' worksheets first to give perspective. Remember that this is the fun bit of each chapter so try to make sure it is enjoyable! Try these challenges out yourself and get involved. Make sure you spend time reflecting on and evaluating both of your efforts!

# Pulling It Together

**Key purpose**: These worksheets are designed to facilitate problem solving in 'real-life' situations, to identify key points of learning from the chapter and to decide if this is an area warranting further action. This process is important for the planning and goal-setting phase that is mapped out in the final chapter.

**User tips**: Go back through all the worksheets in the chapter and together reflect on what has been discovered so that there is a unified picture of needs and priorities. If there is a disagreement as to areas of concern, try to acknowledge everyone's opinions in writing (e.g. when completing the worksheet 'Identifying Goals: Mind Map' p.188, under each identified area write down who has raised it – the young person, adult or both).

# Top Tips

**Key purpose**: 'Top Tips' are divided into separate sheets for young people and adults. They provide additional information, practical considerations and guidance on implementation.

**User tips**: It is recommended that you read these before starting each chapter as they contain 'extra' information that might help to guide you and the young person. They can be particularly helpful when working on developing specific goals or strategies. Some tip sheets have been designed for use as general 'information' sheets to help educate others.

# Resources

**Key purpose**: These lists of additional resources have been added as they may help guide further exploration or support in a particular area. Although they are not all ADHD specific, they are considered highly suitable for supporting young people with attention deficits.

**User tips**: These lists are NOT exclusive – there are other great resources around! Make sure you research any products first in order to check if they will meet your specific needs.

**HOW TO CREATE LEARNING SESSIONS**

## General hints

- Adult support needs to be provided for the completion of worksheets, and reflection on their content, in order to ensure learning and best determine effective strategies.

- Photocopy worksheets to create folders – one each for the adult and young person.

- Try using structure, rewards and breaks during work sessions.

- Balance 'Detect and Reflect' worksheets with 'Give It A Go' so there is always a practical element to each session.

- Use multiple methods to complete worksheets – scribing (e.g. you write while having a discussion as the young person is jumping on a mini-trampoline), using pictures, or typing onto a computer/laptop and printing and pasting in.

- Set your own pace for completing the worksheets to reflect the time available to you.

- Photocopy the 'Reflections' form at the end of this chapter in 'Top Tips'. At the end of each session quickly note your thoughts; either by adding the ideas to the one form for each chapter, or (if you like writing!) you can use the sheet on a session-by-session basis.

- Photocopy the 'My To Do List' form at the end of the chapter and use this with the young person to set homework tasks and as a prompt sheet on what to bring to the next session.

- Be creative and add your own touches to the sessions!

## Chapter order

- You can change the order of chapters to some degree. However, the 'Surviving Homework!' chapter does rely on information and strategies learnt through the completion of 'Don't Miss A Thing!' and 'Getting Sorted'.

- We recommend that even if a young person does not have problems in one area (e.g. 'Friends and Mates') it can be very powerful to have them complete that chapter. This positively reinforces relative strengths that they can take pride in and build on.

## Group sessions

Groups can be an effective way of teaching the skills from this book in a social context. They can also provide additional motivation and promote shared learning and problem solving. There are so many possible formats and settings in which you could run groups from this programme that we cannot provide definitive advice. However, our experience recommends that you:

- consider the ratio of staff to young people; keep the group small (maximum of four is ideal) and ensure adequate staff and space to support withdrawal if required

- use motivating positive reward systems (e.g. for effort, contribution, self-calming)

- complete some of the 'Detect and Reflect' worksheets as a group to create variety and facilitate discussion; use a whiteboard, poster or projector to provide visual support

- set some worksheets as homework between sessions

- utilize strategies you have learnt within the sessions, such as fidgets, visual timetables, regular exercise breaks and positive feedback/praise systems

- encourage food breaks to provide opportunities for sharing interests (e.g. play CDs, swap cards) and provide a natural opportunity to model/practise social skills.

## TURNING STRATEGIES INTO ACTION

The final chapter recommends a process for implementing strategies in a way that includes the young person as a partner in working towards simple and achievable goals. It is up to you to decide whether goals are decided and worked on at the same time as you continue to work through this book (e.g. strategies from 'Feeling Great!' and 'Don't Miss A Thing!' chapters are implemented while also working through the remaining chapters). Alternatively, you can complete the entire workbook before goals and strategies are selected. This decision will depend on a variety of factors including your available resources, the relative need/urgency of issues and the time frames involved.

## GETTING STARTED FOR ADULTS

The next few worksheets will take YOU through some important reflections and activities that will help to guide your own learning during this process. The adults around the young person – the parents, teachers and support staff – are often THE MOST POWERFUL influences on determining positive outcomes. These young people need all the help they can get! So the more that we can all learn about ADHD, strive to understand these young individuals and establish habits of actively reflecting on our own beliefs and actions, the better their future will be.

**You have just finished 'Introducing' for Chapter 1 and now it's over to you to try to 'Detect and Reflect' and then 'Give It A Go'. Finish off with 'Pulling It Together', some 'Top Tips' and 'Resources' and a relaxing cup of tea or coffee – you will have earned it!**

# The Big Issues

What do you think are the main areas of strength for your young person with ADHD?

From your perspective, what do you think are the main areas of concern for this young person?

How would you rate your knowledge of ADHD, how it impacts on young people and how to provide support?

List strategies and adaptations that you already know are effective in supporting the young person. Are these used consistently?

# Turning Labels into Understanding

It is easy to list the many challenging behaviours demonstrated by young people with ADHD. However, this labelling sometimes leads us to forget about the young person's experience and the actual *causes* of the behaviour. Highlight any of the behaviour labels demonstrated by the young person you support and then tick the possible experiences you feel might underpin this.

| Behaviour label | What the child may be Experiencing |
| --- | --- |
| Ignoring instructions | ☐ Brain can't tune in to what you are saying<br>☐ Can't work out a plan of where to start<br>☐ Has forgotten and is too embarrassed to ask |
| Snatching objects | ☐ Sees and acts without thinking<br>☐ Wants to start activity/ explore |
| Refusing | ☐ Impulsive response to indicate that is not interested in a task<br>☐ Trying to hide confusion/ lack of understanding<br>☐ Doesn't want to fail or look stupid |
| Talking back | ☐ Speaks before thinking then can't back out<br>☐ Doesn't know how to fix the situation |
| Attention seeking | ☐ Impulsive behaviour –thinks and then does!<br>☐ Has learnt that 'bad' behaviour earns attention/ is rewarding |
| Lies | ☐ Speaks before thinking then can't back out<br>☐ Can't explain a behaviour (impulse) so 'creates' a reason |
| Easily bored | ☐ Loses concentration easily<br>☐ Needs lots of stimulation |
| Doesn't want help | ☐ Doesn't want to look stupid<br>☐ Is able to do the task and doesn't need help |

# Find Your Inner ADHD

We all have very individual preferences and tolerances, and everyone will struggle at times with concentration, impulse control and restlessness. Each of us develops our own coping strategies and we modify our life accordingly. By identifying your own needs, and thinking about how you deal with them, you can better understand and empathize with the young person with ADHD. So answer the following questions to increase your self-awareness:

1.  What do you do to stay awake and remain focused during a long meeting or presentation? What would happen if someone made you sit perfectly still?

2.  How do you cope in hectic environments like a busy shop in a major city where you can't block out the competing stimuli of sights, sounds and smells? Can you stay focused? Do you get stressed? Are you at your best? Do you ever get tired/give up?

3.  When you concentrate on paperwork or read a book, do you need to be in a quiet environment or do you like having background noise? How do you cope when it is the opposite of what you prefer?

4.  Where do you work best – in a messy, busy environment or with everything tidy and surfaces clear? Do you like to have things out where you can see them or put away? How do you cope when it is the opposite of what you prefer?

5.  How many things do you do in your life that you are bad at? Do you typically try and avoid these (e.g. job choice, sharing chores)? When you have to do something you are not good at, how do you feel and what do you do (e.g. avoid/act the clown/rush)?

6.  Take note of all the thoughts that you have in your head. What would people think if you couldn't control your impulses and said these out loud? Do these impulsive thoughts really reflect who you are/your values/your knowledge of rules?

Compare your responses to those of your friends and colleagues. You might be surprised!

# Welcome

Look back through the worksheets you have completed to help answer the questions below.

**Three things that you can congratulate yourself on for already knowing/doing:**

1. _____

2. _____

3. _____

**Three new points of learning or reflection:**

1. _____

2. _____

3. _____

# My To Do List

TASKS TO DO AT HOME:

| Date given: | Tasks: | Date due: |
|---|---|---|
|  |  |  |

THINGS TO BRING TO THE NEXT SESSION: (Use as a checklist for packing your bag)

| 1. Tasks completed at home (see list above) ☐ |
|---|
|  |

NEXT SESSION:

| Day and date | Time | Venue |
|---|---|---|
|  |  |  |

# Five Things Everyone Needs to Know About Helping Young People with ADHD

### 1.   Understanding is the key

- Learn about ADHD, and how it impacts on the young person and life from their viewpoint.

- Remember to always consider the WHY behind actions; their difficulties are genuine!

- Strive to educate others and share positive stories and solutions.

### 2.   Adapt the environment around the young person

- Adjust your expectations and demands, as you would for anyone with special needs.

- Add routine and structure to provide external support around the young person.

- Make a real difference by giving short tasks with a definite end point, frequent breaks (with movement), clear structure, supportive visual aids and reduced distractions.

- Make sure there are regular opportunities for success, enjoyment and positive feedback.

### 3.   Teach skills

- Provide a supportive and positive environment for the practice and learning of skills.

- Help develop strategies to maximize concentration, identify and respond to stress, promote organization, make and keep friends, and develop a healthy self-esteem.

### 4.   Make the young person an active partner

- Discuss individual strengths and difficulties in an open, positive and constructive way.

- Involve them in making decisions, implementing strategies and evaluation.

- Link things to their own goals and priorities – make it meaningful and motivating!

**23**

5. **Consider changes to the system!**

- The strategies used to support young people with ADHD are great for *all individuals*.

- These principles have been successfully adopted in schools, classrooms and families.

# Effective Communication

Young people with ADHD have significant problems with functional, day-to-day communication. This is largely due to their difficulties focusing on key stimuli, processing information (particularly auditory) and organizing information. Key tips for effective communication include:

*Secure and keep their attention:*

- **Change aspects of the sensory environment** to get their attention (e.g. clap, create silence, sound an alarm, flick the lights, change voice pitch/melody).
- **Vary your tone** of voice in order to keep their attention and interest.
- Use **multi-media devices** (e.g. video, interactive software, laser pointers) to create novelty, variety and utilize multiple sensory pathways.

*Keep it simple:*

- **Don't overload them with words**: use short sentences, frequent pauses and stress key words.
- Give the young person extra **time to process requests and respond**. Avoid jumping in and repeating the instructions/adding extra information too quickly.
- **Break instructions into clear steps**, and information into clear topics. Consider giving instructions one at a time rather than all at the very beginning of a task.

*Help them to remember:*

- Reinforce spoken words with **visual supports** (e.g. gestures, lists/bullet points, point to objects, list off steps on your fingers).
- Ask them to **repeat back** the instructions or key pieces of information.

*Keep them engaged and motivated*:

- Use **humour** and have fun.

- **Develop rapport** – show interest in their likes and find opportunities for praise.

- **Phrase things positively** by stating what you want the young person to do (e.g. instead of saying 'Stop daydreaming', say 'Now it is time to finish this worksheet').

- Use your **tone of voice** as an effective tool in helping to regulate the young person's attention and mood. When they need perking up, make your voice fun, energetic, firm and varied. When they need calming down or soothing, keep it warm, quiet and steady without signs of frustration or stress.

*Make them an active partner in communication*:

- Give them more control by providing **clear end points and warnings** (e.g. count down to the finish, give the next 1–2 steps).

- Build in **opportunities for choice** where possible (e.g. for the young person to decide what order to do things, providing a chance for choice/preferred task after a set task).

- **Avoid forcing decisions**. In times of potential difficulty, remind the young person of their options (positively – without any values attached or implied threat) and then give them time and space to consider and respond.

- Acknowledge and reflect back the feelings expressed by the young person by using **active listening** (e.g. 'It sounds like…you are feeling really frustrated'; 'From what I am hearing…you really don't want to be doing this right now'). You might need to respond to the non-verbal cues and expressed emotions rather than the actual content of what they are saying. This enables the young person to more accurately realize what they are in fact feeling and communicating (supports greater insight) and lets them know that this has been acknowledged and considered by the adult.

# Reflections

CHAPTER _____

| | |
|---|---|
| Points of learning for young person: | Points of learning for me: |
| Things to explore/follow up on/research: | Things with potential to work well: |
| Strengths/positives: | Things to share with other people: |
| Other observations/issues: | |

# Welcome

## BOOKS – INFORMATION AND STRATEGIES

- *The Source for ADD/ADHD* by Gail J. Richard and Joy L. Russell, 2001, Lingui Systems.
- *Attention Deficit Hyperactivity Disorder: The Latest Assessment and Treatment Strategies (3rd Edition)* by C. Keith Conners, PhD, 2006, Compact Clinicians.
- *How to Reach and Teach Teenagers with ADHD* by Grad Flick, 2000, Jossey Bass.
- *Teenagers with ADD and ADHD: A Guide for Parents and Professionals* by Chris Zeigler Dendy, 2005, Woodbine House Inc.

## BOOKS – VIEWS FROM YOUNG PEOPLE/FAMILIES AND STRATEGIES

- *A Bird's-Eye View of Life with ADD and ADHD: Advice from Young Survivors* by Chris Zeigler Dendy, 2007, Cherish the Children.
- *Marching to a Different Tune: Diary about an ADHD Boy* by Jacky Fletcher, 1999, Jessica Kingsley Publishers.
- *The ADHD Parenting Handbook: Practical Advice for Parents from Parents* by Colleen Roberts, 1994, Taylor Trade Publishing.
- *ADHD and ME: What I Learned from Lighting Fires at the Dinner Table* by Blake Taylor, 2008, New Harbinger Publications.

## INTERNET SITES

- ADDISS (ADHD Information Services): www.addiss.co.uk
- ADDERS ADD/ADHD Online Support Group: www.adders.org
- National Resource Center on ADHD: www.help4adhd.org
- ADD in School: www.addinschool.com/highschool.htm
- Children and Adults with Attention Deficit/Hyperactivity Disorder: www.chadd.org

# Getting Started

## WHAT YOU NEED TO KNOW

This workbook is written and designed for young people with ADHD – people just like you. It is hoped that it will help you discover and practise different ideas that can help you at school. Some of the ideas will also be helpful in other parts of your life such as home, at the shops, at sports practice or even on the bus. This book can be used at any time, but may be extra helpful around the time of moving on to a new school.

This book might be a little different to some others that you have seen. We (the authors) have worked with lots of young people with ADHD, and they have helped us to figure out a few things, such as:

1.  You already know a lot of stuff about yourself, like some of the things that work well for you and some of the things that don't.

2.  The people close to you at home and school also have lots of great information about you and your skills.

3.  Teamwork between you and the people helping you is important – you all need to be involved in decisions, making plans, changing things and trying them out.

4.  Changes don't just happen overnight – things need to be researched, tested and perfected. This is no different from designing, producing and marketing a new version of a computer game.

5.  It is good to have some fun while thinking and learning!

Each chapter in this book has a specific topic to work through. Within each chapter, there are different types of worksheets for you to complete; some of these ask you to survey people you know, others ask you to write or draw about your experiences and some will give you special tasks to test out.

There are three young people who will work with you and keep you entertained throughout the book. Here's your chance to meet them:

Hi! I'm Carly. I am 12 years old and my favourite things are probably music and hip-hop dancing. I spend my weekends hanging out with friends and playing hockey. I was diagnosed with ADD a few years ago – it took people a while to figure it out because I'm not 'hyperactive' like others can be. I guess my biggest stress at the moment is that when I start high school next year, some of my friends will be at a different school.

Hey, how are you? My name is James; I am 10 and like heaps of stuff. I like playing with my dog Ferris, climbing trees, playing on my computer and pulling pranks. I am going to move schools later this year and I am a bit worried about it, especially because I just found out I have ADHD.

Everyone calls me Zac. I am 14 and like basketball, especially trying out new tricks and moves. At school, my favourite subjects are woodwork and metalwork and I am thinking about becoming a builder or maybe a mechanic. I was diagnosed with ADHD ages ago, and at first I was really angry. I didn't want any help or even to go to the doctors. But now I have kind of got used to it.

*A good tip from Zac:*
Photocopy the worksheets from this book and then put them in a folder to make your own 'book' (one chapter at a time). It might be a good idea to buy a special folder and make a cool beginning title page using clipart or Photoshop. The grown-up who you will be working with might also want their own folder and title page. They might need you to help them with the technical stuff!

*Carly wants to mention:*
It doesn't matter what type of ADHD or ADD you have – this workbook is designed for everyone! But we have just used the term 'ADHD' to keep things simple. We have also chosen to use the term 'high school' to describe senior schools, but we know that if you are living in different parts of the world it might be called something else.

**Have fun getting started!**

# ADHD: Fact and Fiction

What do you think it means to have ADHD? Write down some words or phrases that make sense to you:

There are LOTS of myths and mistakes out there about ADHD. Look at the list below and cross out the myths – those things NOT linked to ADHD. Circle the things that are correct. Once you have finished, talk about your ideas and check the answer sheet in 'Top Tips' at the end of this chapter.

| | | |
|---|---|---|
| Trouble staying focused | Being stupid | Speaking before thinking |
| Need to move and fidget | Being naughty | Being cool |
| Just want attention | Forget things | Not trying hard enough |
| Mental/crazy/a freak | Nothing will help | Just have too much sugar |
| Find some school stuff hard | Can't sit still | Medication is the only answer |

How accurate was your 'myth detection'?

# We Are All Unique

Everyone is unique; this means that people are different to look at (except identical twins!), have different personalities, and are good at and need help with different things. You may know people who need help with reading, wear glasses, have allergies, or have ADHD or asthma. Think about what makes you unique, and in particular the things you find easy to do and the things you find more difficult. Fill in the table below – James has already made a start to give you some ideas.

| What things are easy and go OK at home and school? | What things are more difficult at home and school? |
| --- | --- |
| Work on the computer<br>Sports lessons | Sitting quietly and reading<br>Spelling tests |

# What the Others Say

Everyone with ADHD is different – an individual! Yet some of the ways that ADHD makes you feel and how it affects your life might be similar to what some other young people go through. Read these quotes from James, Carly and Zac about having ADHD and use a highlighter to mark any bits that are like things you have felt.

 I like having lots of energy, talking lots and I'm always joking and doing fun things. It's annoying that some things seem harder for me than other kids. Sometimes even when I try really hard I just can't get my head to stay on track and get things finished. I reckon it feels like there is an engine in me going flat out. I get myself in trouble sometimes too… I am always being told off!

I think of ADD like this – some parts of my brain don't work the same way as other people's. It still works, of course! But the bits that help me concentrate and help me think things through don't work as well. Sometimes I say things that I want to take back. I tend to forget things as well. I sit in class and daydream a lot!

 ADHD is just a part of me, like having curly hair and liking pizza. It's tough sometimes, but I am lucky I am good at lots of things like making stuff and playing basketball. I do need extra help at school, and I take medication as well. I used to hate this at first but now it is OK and I can see how it helps.

# Transition: A Trip Down Memory Lane

This worksheet will help you to find out what someone else remembers about changing schools. Ask a parent, carer, relative, teacher or neighbour if you can interview them. You want to ask about what it was like for them when they moved to a new school, especially when they first moved to high school, so use the questions below.

1.   Why did you change school and how old were you?

2.   How did you feel on your first day at your new school?

3.   What did you like about your new school?

4.   What was hard about starting at the school?

5.   Can you remember your favourite teachers and why?

6.   What were your best and worst subjects?

7.   Did you ever get into trouble at school? If so, what for?

8.   Share something really embarrassing that happened at high school.

# Transition: All Change!

Changing schools or classes can leave you with lots of different feelings, such as happiness, excitement, worry, sadness or even all of these! Complete this worksheet to detect and reflect on your feelings about your old and your new school or class.

What three things will you miss about your *old* school or class?

1. _____

2. _____

3. _____

What three things won't you miss about your *old* school or class?

1. _____

2. _____

3. _____

What three things are you looking forward to about your *new* school or class?

1. _____

2. _____

3. _____

What three things are you worried about at your *new* school or class?

1. _____

2. _____

3. _____

# You Are Not Alone!

Have a look at these internet sites or at any books on ADHD you can find:

- answers to questions about ADD/ADHD: www.addvance.com/help/teens
- National Resource Center on ADHD: www.help4adhd.org/en/living/ parenting/teeninfo (then click on link 'What is ADHD anyway?')
- support and advice for teens with ADHD: www.teenadders.org.nz/ treatment.htm#add

Read what they say about ADHD and write down:

One new thing you have learnt:            One thing you found interesting:

Now imagine you are on an ADHD website and you see that someone has posted the message below. What would you write back? Have a go at writing a response below.

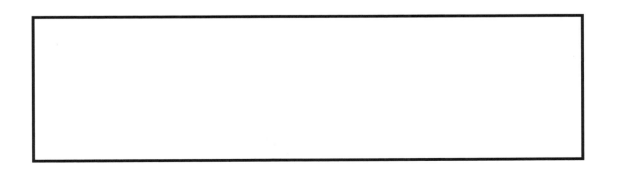

'Hi. Feeling really confused at moment. Just went to some doctor who said I have ADHD. Not sure what to think – he talked to my Mum about taking tablets for it which seems weird. I don't know anyone with ADHD… I just wish I'd never gone to that doctor.'

# Be the Expert

You can be the expert about yourself and your ADHD! Look through any resources you have on ADHD, including other work or tip sheets, books or the internet. Then make a PowerPoint presentation on ADHD. Try to use the following format, but of course you can add extra things if you want to!

| | |
|---|---|
| Slide 1: Title page<br><br>(insert a photo of you or a cool picture from the internet) | Slide 2: Three main symptoms of ADHD |
| Slide 3: Three good things about ADHD + two famous people with ADHD | Slide 4: Three things that ADHD makes difficult for YOU |

Remember to choose a slide design that you like. You can also change the colour scheme and add pictures and animations.

Once you have finished your PowerPoint, arrange a time with your family to sit down and show them. You can even turn it into a 'special' event and send invitations, arrange seats like at the movies and have popcorn.

Maybe you could also invite other people who are close to you – grandparents, family friends or neighbours?

# Transition: Private Investigator

It is a good idea to find out as much as possible about your new school or class before you start. There are lots of ways you can do this – you might be able to read through their brochure, look on their website, visit the school/class or talk to people you know who already go to the school. See if you can find out some of the answers to the questions below when doing your research!

1. What time does school start? _____

2. What time does school finish? _____

3. When is registration/form time/home room? _____

4. What subjects will you be studying? _____

   _____

5. What is the food like in the school café/canteen? _____

6. Are you allowed to take mobile/cell phones into school? _____

7. Name one teacher at the school who seems nice? _____

8. What happens if homework isn't completed on time? _____

9. What times are the breaks? _____

10. Who could you talk to if you needed help at school? _____

# Getting Started

Look back through the worksheets you have completed to help answer the questions below.

**Three new things you have learnt about ADHD:**

1. _____

2. _____

3. _____

**Some questions you have about ADHD or ADD:**

1. _____

2. _____

# ADHD: Fact and Fiction Answer Sheet

## FACT

- Trouble staying focused (problems concentrating is a big feature of ADHD).
- Forget things (people with ADHD often leave things behind and forget deadlines).
- Speaking before thinking (this is part of what is called 'impulsivity').
- Can't sit still (part of hyperactivity, so it might not be a 'fact' for you if you have ADD).
- Need to move and fidget (part of hyperactivity, so it might not be true if you have ADD).
- Find some school stuff hard (ADHD makes school work hard, no matter how smart you are!).

## FICTION

- Not trying hard enough (ADHD is not about being lazy or not trying!).
- Being stupid (ADHD has nothing to do with how smart you are).
- Just have too much sugar (sugar does not cause ADHD, but cutting back sometimes helps!).
- Being naughty (people get confused because some of the challenges created by ADHD can make people look like they are being 'naughty', even when they are not).
- Just want attention (no-one chooses to have ADHD – you have it or you don't!).
- Mental/crazy/a freak (there is nothing strange about ADHD: everyone is different and everyone has different ways of thinking; girls and boys are different; people who are good at sport are different to people who are good at music, but this doesn't make us freaks!).
- Nothing will help (there are plenty of ways of helping, even if they take time and practice).
- Medication is the only answer (medication can really help some people, but it is not the *only* way to help your ADHD; other strategies always need to be used as well).

AND 'BEING COOL' IS UP TO YOU!

# Understanding ADHD

ADHD has three main features – hyperactivity, poor impulse control and reduced attention. Some people have what is called the 'inattentive' type of ADHD, called ADD, which means they have poor impulse control and reduced attention but do not have the hyperactivity.

### BUT WHAT DOES THIS REALLY MEAN?

| | |
|---|---|
| **REDUCED ATTENTION** 1 | Young people with ADHD say that reduced attention is like:<br>• finding it really hard to focus on the thing you are doing or meant to be doing<br>• feeling like your eyes, ears and mind jump from one thing to the next<br>• noticing everything that is happening around you all the time<br>• finding it hard sometimes to 'pull away' your focus from one task, even when you need to listen or look at something else<br>• finding it really hard to keep going until something is finished<br>• finding it impossible to do something and listen at the same time. |
| **POOR IMPULSE CONTROL** 2 | Young people with ADHD say that poor impulse control is when you:<br>• say things and do things before you think<br>• have problems waiting for your turn in an activity or a conversation<br>• sometimes break the rules without even thinking about it or realizing it<br>• see something and need to touch it, even if you shouldn't<br>• want to get to the answer straight away<br>• rush into things really quickly and don't make a plan. |

| | |
|---|---|
| **HYPERACTIVITY**<br> | Young people with ADHD say that hyperactivity can be like:<br><br>• always wanting to move<br>• needing to keep changing how you are sitting – rocking on the chair, wrapping your legs around the chair legs, tucking feet up onto the seat<br>• talking too much or making noises with your mouth<br>• chewing on things or putting things in your mouth<br>• touching and fiddling with things. |
| **BONUS STUFF!**<br> | Young people with ADHD might have problems with ORGANIZATION like:<br><br>• forgetting things and leaving things behind<br>• struggling to plan ahead and work out the order of steps for what needs to get done<br>• never knowing where things are and never having a routine<br>• always seeming to be in chaos!<br>Young people with ADHD also have some real TALENTS like:<br><br>• having lots of energy<br>• being really enthusiastic and passionate about the things they like<br>• learning well by doing things and making things<br>• being creative and thinking in a different way. |

# Transition to High School

**Tips while still at the old school:**

- Start skill development at least a year before the move, targeting topics such as those covered in this book. Work towards strategies that promote independence and that can be directly transferred into a high school setting.

- Involve the family in skill development and planning; teaching can be shared across the home and school and strategies practised in multiple settings.

- Consider referrals to specialists for consultation and support.

- Familiarize the young person with the changes they can expect in order to 'de-mystify' the process, remembering that information typically reduces anxiety!

- Clearly document all of the *successful* strategies that have been used to support the young person either currently or in the recent past. Include effective approaches for issues such as setting up the classroom, interaction, providing hands-on support, teaching, behaviour management, social support and working with parents/carers.

- Use methods of documentation that will ensure information is easily accessible for the new teaching staff (e.g. transition handover summary sheet in this chapter).

**Ideas on collaborative working between both schools and the family:**

- Hold at least one meeting before transition, with both schools and the family present.

- Identify the key areas of predicted need during the transition and together make concrete plans around how to support this.

- Hold a follow-up meeting after transition, with both schools and the family present. This ensures knowledge is not lost and allows for solution-focused problem solving.

**Tips for the new school:**

- Create a 'team' of key staff members who will act as a support network for the young person.

- Have the student visit the school before starting so they can meet their support network and other key people (e.g. principal, administration staff) and know their way around.

- Develop systems for communication between the key stakeholders:

- systems for communicating between teachers: strategies and goals, what to do, what is working well, where the problems are (e.g. staff meetings, 'student profile' in staff room)

- systems for communicating between the school and family (e.g. schedule weekly ten-minute meetings or phone calls to avoid crisis-only contact or missed calls)

- systems for communicating between professionals involved (e.g. two-monthly meetings between all stakeholders to review the case, swap ideas and coordinate planning and support).

• Organize staff training and professional development on understanding ADHD and in practical management strategies. Reinforce this learning using worksheets from this book.

• Continue with active skill development and specialized support for the young person.

**Ways to help at home:**

• Avoid 'passing on' any of your worries about the transition; stay calm and confident!

• Purchase new uniforms/books/diaries early so the young person can get familiarized.

• Visit the new school during holidays and/or weekends to help them get to know where things are (e.g. toilets, office, sports hall).

• Write down the strategies that work well for you at home and share these with the new school. Also let them know what is hard at home so they see the big picture.

• Arrange a special event to mark changing schools, like a party, trip or favourite meal.

# Handover Summary Sheet For Transition

| TRANSITION/HANDOVER SUMMARY SHEET FOR: |
| --- |
| Identified needs/diagnosis: |
| Areas of strength and interest: |
| Works best when: |
| Current level and type of support provided at school: |

Other agencies supporting:

Effective strategies – past and current:

Perceived challenges for transition:

Recommended areas/skills to develop:

Written by:

Date:

# Getting Started

## BOOKS ON ADHD FOR YOUNG PEOPLE

- *I Would If I Could: A Teenager's Guide to ADHD* by Michael Gordon, 1991, Atlantic Books.
- *Putting on the Brakes: A Young People's Guide to Understanding ADHD* by Patricia Quinn and Judith Stern, 2001, Magination Press.
- *A Bird's-Eye View of Life with ADD and ADHD: Advice from Young Survivors* by Chris Zeigler Dendy, 2007, Cherish the Children.
- *The Survival Guide for Kids with ADD or ADHD* by John Taylor, 2006, Free Spirit Publishing Inc.
- *ADHD – Living without Brakes* by Martin Kutscher, 2008, Jessica Kingsley Publishers.
- *Cory Stories: A Kid's Book About Living with ADHD* by Jeanne Kraus, 2005, Magination Press.

## BOOKS ON TRANSITION FOR YOUNG PEOPLE

- *It's Your Move! Your Guide to Moving to Secondary School* by Nick Harding, 2006, Scripture Union Publishing.

## BOOKS AND INTERNET SITES ON ADHD FOR ADULTS

- See 'Resources' section of the 'Welcome' chapter.

## BOOKS ON TRANSITION FOR ADULTS

- *Moving to Secondary School: Advice and Activities to Support Transition* by Lynda Measor with Mike Fleetham, 2005, Network Educational Press Ltd.

# CHAPTER 3

# Feeling Great!
# Self-Esteem

Self-esteem is a key component in creating and maintaining emotional wellbeing. A young person with good self-esteem will feel worthwhile, loveable, competent and proud of themselves. Young people with low self-esteem often believe that they aren't valued by others, and that they aren't able or good enough to do certain tasks. They are also more likely to experience difficulties in forming relationships and may find it more difficult to deal with the challenges of life.

Although a person's self-esteem develops throughout their lifetime, the foundations are laid in childhood. For young people, the messages given to them by the important adults in their lives directly influence their sense of self-worth and capability. If these messages are predominantly positive then the young person begins to internalize the positive concepts of self-worth and capability, relying less on others for approval. This young person is more likely to give tasks a go, believe that they are loveable and recognize their own 'good' qualities. This outlook will help them deal with many of the challenges that they may face throughout their lifetime.

## ADHD AND SELF-ESTEEM

Children and young people with ADHD are typically more vulnerable to experiencing low self-esteem. Throughout their childhood they are likely to have been faced with repeated negative messages about their behaviour, participation and learning. This criticism, combined with their actual experiences of failure at home, school and in social settings, may lead them to feel negatively about themselves and develop low self-esteem. In turn, this can lead to a range of secondary problems as they attempt to navigate life. For example, the young person may not put effort into tasks and activities in which they expect to fail. They may seek social acceptance using undesirable means (e.g. breaking rules, swearing) and they may try to mask their difficulties by acting the clown or withdrawing/avoiding.

## CHALLENGES AT HIGH SCHOOL

Strong self-esteem is important during periods of change, such as when transferring schools. It is recognized that for all young people, even those without additional needs, the move to a new school can be challenging enough to reduce self-esteem. Therefore, it is even more important that young people with ADHD receive active support in this area ahead of any change. A more positive self-image will be a valuable resilience factor in helping them cope with the stresses of the first few months in their new school.

It is also important to recognize that, during the teenage years, peers become an increasingly influential factor in a young person's self-esteem. Therefore it becomes even more important to facilitate positive social networks and friendships, and to avoid negative experiences such as bullying (see the 'Friends and Mates' chapter).

## OBJECTIVES

The worksheets in this chapter are designed to support the following processes:

- To help the young person reflect on their self-image and their own areas of strength and challenge.

- To explore and try out strategies that can help to promote good self-esteem.

- To help the young person identify strategies that work for them and that might be helpful in daily life.

# I Am...

1.  How do you feel about yourself? Rate how you feel on a scale of 1–10:

10   9   8   7   6   5   4   3   2   1

I am a good person                                   I am a bad person

10   9   8   7   6   5   4   3   2   1

I am a fun person                                    I am a boring person

10   9   8   7   6   5   4   3   2   1

I am a likeable person                        Nobody likes me as a person

2.  What do you think is the most important?

☐ Being the best          OR      ☐ Trying your best

☐ Winning                 OR      ☐ Not giving up

☐ Being really popular    OR      ☐ Having a few really good friends

Ask two other people what they think and ask them: WHY?

3.  Can you think of any people from movies or TV who learnt that winning and
    being popular is NOT always the most important thing?

# I Am Cool!/I Love Me!/I Rock!

Choose one of these titles (I am cool!/I love me!/I rock!) or make one of your own. Write it at the top of your list below, and then put down all the things you like about yourself. Also ask your parents and the people that know you to add some of the things that they like about you to your list.

# All About Me

Fill in the circle below to create a profile of you as a unique person. What things do you like doing or eating? What is your personality like – are you kind, fun, moody? What things don't you like doing or eating? What are your top five movies or computer games? What do you look like – hair, eyes, clothes style? What's good about having ADHD?

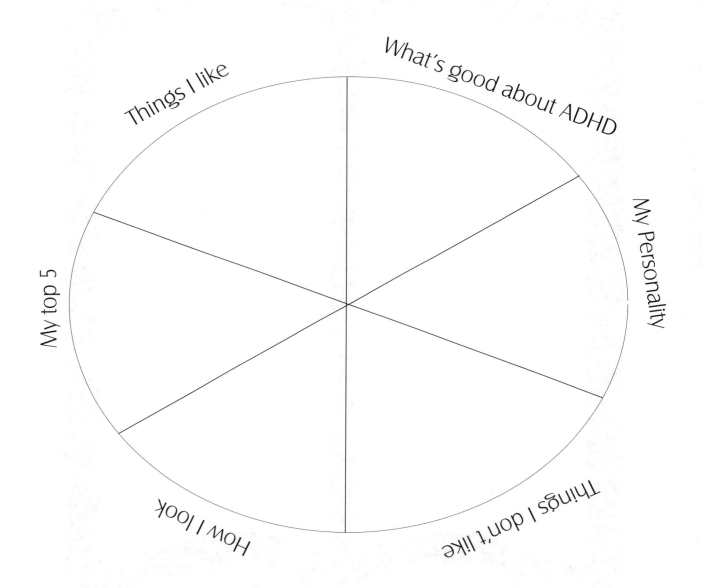

# Three Wishes

Imagine that you have been given three wishes that you can use to change things about yourself. What three things would you change? Write your wishes below:

1.

2.

3.

# Be Your Hero

Think of your favourite hero. They might be from a book or movie, or they might be a sports star or someone famous. First, work out how your hero would think, act, walk and talk. Then pretend that you are your hero for five minutes and try to do things just as they would, for example talk to a friend, make a sandwich or play a board game. You can do this by yourself or with someone else who is also pretending to be their hero.

Have a quick discussion on the following:

- How did it feel to think, act and talk like your hero?
  What was different?

- Would thinking or acting like this be helpful at any times (e.g. when faced with a problem, when feeling upset, when learning something new)?

# Compliments: The Family Challenge

Sometimes we are so busy rushing around that we forget to tell the important people in our lives when they do something well or when they are helpful, kind or fun. So ask your family if they will take on this 'family challenge' over the next week. Each person has to give everyone else in the family two compliments a day. For example, you might say to your Mum or Dad, 'Thanks for my dinner, it tasted delicious', or to your brother or sister, 'Thanks for waiting for me to finish on the computer; it was a really nice thing to do.'

A good rule of thumb when giving someone a compliment is to try and include two parts:

| | | | | |
|---|---|---|---|---|
| **What they did** | **+** | **Why it was good** | **=** | **The perfect compliment!** |

Some examples are:

| What they did | Why it was good | The perfect compliment! |
|---|---|---|
| 'Thanks for…getting me a drink/letting me choose the DVD/helping with my work/listening to me whinge.' | 'It was really… kind/thoughtful/ hard working/ generous/funny/ friendly/fun.' | 'Thanks for giving the family challenge a go and finding good things to say about everyone. It was really impressive!' |

- Put a copy of this on the fridge to remind everyone – copy it onto bright paper so it stands out!
- At the end of the week, fill in the table on the next page to see how everyone got on with the family challenge. Remember to give compliments for trying!

# The Family Challenge: How Did We Go?

| Name of family member | Example of a compliment given (and who they gave it to) | Did they pass the challenge? | Did they like the challenge? |
|---|---|---|---|
| 1 | | | |
| 2 | | | |
| 3 | | | |
| 4 | | | |
| 5 | | | |

# Positive Self-Talk

It is important to learn how to encourage yourself when faced with a difficult task. Sometimes, things like hard homework assignments, helping with housework or going to see a teacher if you are in trouble can be really daunting.

One way of dealing with this is to say positive, helpful things to yourself. Sportsmen and women use this trick all the time so they play to their best and don't give up when things get difficult. It may be useful to make a flashcard with a couple of phrases on it to help as a reminder. You can keep these in your wallet, pencil case or diary. Here are some phrases that other people have found useful. Try and think of two of your own and write them in the thought bubbles below.

# I Can Do It! I've Already Done It!

Think about a time when you were faced with a real challenge in your life. It might have been something that happened at home like moving towns, someone getting sick or a time when you did something really stupid (and got into trouble!). Or it could have been something at school, like trying out for a team, making new friends or giving a talk/presentation. Write one of the challenges you have faced here:

_____

Spend some time thinking about how you coped with this. What did you do? What did you think? Did you get any extra help? How did you cope? Draw or write about that time below:

Have a good look at the things that helped you get through. They might be things that you can do again in the future when challenges appear!

**WELL DONE!**

# What Could I Do If...?

Imagine yourself in the situations below. Think about how you might respond using the ideas you have learnt from this chapter of the book.

**Situation 1:**

You overhear a couple of people in your class saying that you are a loser and have no friends. You try to ignore them but that night you keep thinking about it and are feeling pretty unhappy. What could you do to help yourself feel better?

_____

_____

_____

_____

**Situation 2:**

Your English teacher asks to see you after school to discuss your homework. She tells you that she can't accept your homework because you didn't answer the questions fully, so you need to do it again. She also lets you know that she thinks your handwriting has improved, but it is still hard to read at times and you need to keep working to make it neater. Write down two different encouraging things you could say to yourself to help you feel OK.

_____

_____

_____

_____

# Feeling Great!

Look back through the worksheets you have completed to help answer the questions below.

**What do I think of me?**
One thing I would never change about me

_____

One thing I would like to change about me

_____

**My top three strategies to help me feel good and cope with challenges!**

1. _____

2. _____

3. _____

## WOULD SELF-ESTEEM BE A GOOD AREA TO WORK ON?

| Young person: | ☐ Yes | ☐ No | ☐ Maybe |
|---|---|---|---|
| Adult: | ☐ Yes | ☐ No | ☐ Maybe |

**If YES or MAYBE, see Chapter 9 for help with goal setting**

# Feeling Great!

Here are some extra tips on how to feel great about yourself and enjoy life:

- **Be kind to yourself!** Make a habit of saying positive things to yourself such as 'I'm good at football', 'I look good today' or 'I tried really hard'. This will then balance out some of the negative things you might think about yourself at times.

- **Find something you are good at and do it more!** Everyone is good at some things and not as good at others. Try to work out what things you are good at and then do them more and more – it will help you to feel happier and more confident.

- **Don't worry about making mistakes.** You can't expect to get everything right all of the time! Most of the mistakes we make help us to learn for next time.

- **It's OK to be different.** ADHD can make some young people feel different to their friends. Just remember there are some good things about having ADHD and that you aren't alone. You might want to think about joining an online group for young people with ADHD.

- **Be realistic** with the things you want to get done and achieve. Try to break down goals into small, achievable 'mini' goals. This way when you complete each 'mini' goal you can enjoy the feeling of success and progress!

- **Help out someone else.** You might help a friend with their sports practice, complete a sponsored activity for charity, make your Mum a cup of coffee or volunteer to help a teacher at lunch time. By helping out others you are making a real difference for them, at the same time as helping yourself feel great!

- **Keep active.** Getting regular exercise not only helps us to be healthy, but also fills our body with 'feel good' chemicals. Being active doesn't always have to be playing sports; it could be going for a walk, dancing in your room, mowing the lawn or digging in the garden.

# Feeling Great!

Here are some simple ways to help boost a young person's self-esteem!

- **Help them to develop an understanding of what ADHD is** and what it means for them. This knowledge can help to prevent them from feeling stupid or feeling bad about the things that they find difficult to do.

- **Provide encouragement and praise** wherever possible – try to catch the young person doing positive things! Compliments do not need to be based on just success, but can also include effort. Praise also needs to be specific (e.g. replace general statements like 'that was good' with 'it was good how you...').

- **Set up a reward system.** Rewarding a young person with stickers, points, small treats or special privileges can be a real boost to their self-esteem. Creating a chart or feedback sheet so that successes can be easily seen and tracked is also likely to be helpful. Make sure any rewards or feedback are given immediately after the positive actions/behaviours so that they connect their success with the reward. NEVER take away rewards that have already been earned but instead find other consequences if they are needed.

- **Give constructive criticism.** There will be times when you do need to explain to a young person that you would like them to do something differently. Try to ensure that when you give this feedback it's delivered in a calm way with the focus on the behaviour that needs to be changed, not the person. If possible, try to balance out the criticism with some positive feedback, and be clear about what behaviour you actually want to see.

- **Avoid comparisons.** Try not to compare the young person with their siblings or friends as this may really dent their self-esteem.

- Provide the young person with **regular opportunities for success**. Encourage them to take part in activities that build on their strengths and interests.

# Feeling Great!

- *Helping Children to Build Self-Esteem: A Photocopiable Activities Book* by Deborah Plummer and Alice Harper, 2007, Jessica Kingsley Publishers.

- *Ideas to Go: Self-Esteem Ages 10–12* by Tanya Dalgleish, 2002, A & C Black Publishers.

- *Self-Esteem Games for Children* by Deborah Plummer, 2006, Jessica Kingsley Publishers.

- *Don't Feed the Monster on Tuesdays! The Children's Self-Esteem Book* by Adolph Moser, 1991, Landmark Editions.

- *The Straight Talk Manual: A Self-Esteem and Life Skills Workbook for Young People (5th Edition)* by Diane Brokenshire, 2001, Straight Talk Publishing.

- *Talkabout Relationships – Building Self-Esteem and Relationship Skills* by Alex Kelly, 2004, Speechmark Publishing Ltd.

# CHAPTER 4

# Don't Miss A Thing! Attention and Concentration

Attention is a person's ability to focus on the most important thing for them at any one time. This skill is surprisingly complex and, as a result, it is easy to underestimate the significant and wide-ranging impact of difficulties in this area. There are many different types of attention, including:

- *Sustained attention*: This is the ability to attend to a routine, repetitive task and to remain focused until the task is completed.

- *Selective attention*: This is the ability to pay attention to the most important thing in the environment, even when there are lots of distractions around.

- *Alternating attention*: This is the ability to move our attention backwards and forwards between tasks in a timely and accurate way.

- *Divided attention*: This is the ability to focus on multiple tasks at the same time. Divided attention is the most complex of attention abilities and very important in daily life.

## ADHD AND ATTENTION

One of the key criteria for a diagnosis of ADHD is to have significant and widespread difficulties with attention abilities. Young people with ADHD often have problems with the majority, if not all, of the attention types listed above. It is important to recognize a few key features of their unique difficulties in this area:

1.  There will be some things that the young person CAN focus on! This does not mean that they are 'faking it' or 'not trying' at other times. Often the activities they can focus on will be computer games, TV/DVDs, sport or specific interests. It is important to recognize that these activities often have very high levels of intense sensory stimulation that aid sustained attention. They may also be highly motivating and exciting. Often you will still be able to see problems with attention around these activities, such as not being able to shift attention away from them (e.g. to answer the phone/hear an instruction) and with dividing their attention (e.g. talking while playing/watching, focusing on all things in an activity – the ball, themselves, their team-mates AND the goal).

2.  Attention will fluctuate from minute to minute and day to day – don't let this frustrate you! The young person does not have control over these neurological and biochemical changes. It is best to always plan for those times when concentration is at its worst.

3.  Attention problems can't be 'fixed'. Attention control is one of the key areas where prescribed medication can have a positive impact and some young people also report improvements in response to dietary changes.

Sensory-based strategies also contribute to some improvements in this skill area. However, it is understood that these measures, or any others taken, will NOT 'fix' difficulties with attention and that additional support is ALWAYS important in supporting young people with ADHD.

4.  We need to meet the young person past the halfway point. Although we can try to improve their ability to concentrate, the most crucial and effective step is to adjust both the environment and the demands on the young person to better meet their current attention abilities and needs.

5.  Other factors will impact on attention and need to be supported alongside the strategies outlined in this chapter. These factors include such things as the young person's cognitive skills (e.g. no-one can focus well on something they don't understand), memory skills (e.g. even when they do focus they may be unable to retain the information) and motor skills (e.g. needing to focus on the handwriting will compromise focus on the content). The individual's ability to focus can be further affected by their restlessness/hyperactivity and impulsiveness, which drive them to continually move, touch things, talk, chew or explore. On top of this, externally driven factors including stress, fatigue and social issues also have a significant impact.

If a young person experiences difficulties with their attention, this can lead to a range of problems including:

- forgetting things – even frequently used items like homework and bus passes
- forgetting instructions for a task (particularly if there are lots of parts)
- difficulties listening to others and knowing when they are being spoken to
- making silly mistakes with things even though they know what to do
- not finishing pieces of work or jobs around the house
- doing what they are not meant to do such as talking to other people in class, drawing/doodling, daydreaming
- becoming quickly bored with activities; changing and flitting between activities
- frequently changing topics during conversations.

## CHALLENGES AT HIGH SCHOOL

At high school the curriculum and teaching methods place significantly greater demands on a student's attention skills. They are expected to remember long and complex instructions, focus for longer times with less 'fun' and 'activity' as well as self-manage their homework, assignments and equipment. There is often significantly less support provided by teachers, and students are expected to have the skills and abilities to complete tasks with greater independence.

## OBJECTIVES

We all experience difficulties with our concentration on occasion, and at these times we use strategies that enable us to concentrate for longer or that re-focus our attention. Similarly, young people with ADHD can be assisted in developing their individual support mechanisms. At the same time, achievable and consistent expectations need to be developed around the young person, based on their existing attention span. External support and structure can be effective in maximizing and supporting greater consistency in the ability to focus (see Tip Sheet – Creating a Good 'Fit').

The worksheets in this chapter are designed to support the following processes:

1. To help the young person learn about their own and other people's attention skills and challenges.

2. To create an opportunity to explore and try out new strategies that might help the young person better manage their attention difficulties.

3. To explore adjustments that can be made in the environment.

4. To help identify strategies that work and that might be helpful in daily life.

# Concentration: Good Times and Tough Times

There will already have been times when you concentrated really well. These were times when you got started, worked through all the steps and actually *finished*! Think of two times when you have done this recently and fill in the table below. James has already started.

**THE GOOD TIMES...**

| Where was I? | What was I doing? | How long did I concentrate for (without any help)? |
|---|---|---|
| In my bedroom | Playing on the PlayStation | 20 minutes |
|  |  |  |
|  |  |  |

There will also have been times when you found that you couldn't concentrate very well. Think about two recent examples and use them to fill in the table below.

**THE TOUGH TIMES...**

| Where was I? | What was I doing? | How long did I concentrate for (without any help)? |
|---|---|---|
| Kitchen table | Writing a poem for English | 3 minutes |
|  |  |  |
|  |  |  |

# The Impact Factor

Do you think that problems with concentration sometimes cause difficulties for you at:

- HOME? (circle answer)          YES / NO
- SCHOOL? (circle answer)        YES / NO

What is the impact of this? Write in the explosion below the things that annoy you about not being able to concentrate, or the things that you seem to find more challenging because you can't always focus. For example, maybe you never seem to get things finished or maybe you always get into trouble for daydreaming.

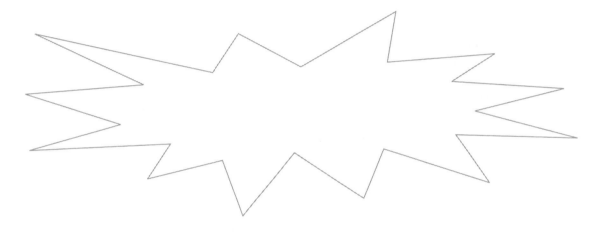

Speak to two people (even better if it can be your teacher plus one of your parents) and find out what they see as being the 'down side' when you are struggling to focus. Write their answers into the explosions below.

# My Distractions

Distractions are things that we notice even when we are trying to focus on something else. They are the things that 'break' our attention and that we find hard to ignore. Here are some examples of the sorts of things that Carly finds distracting. Shade in or highlight any of these that fit for you and add some of your own ideas in the blank shapes.

**SEEING things and LOOKING AT things:**

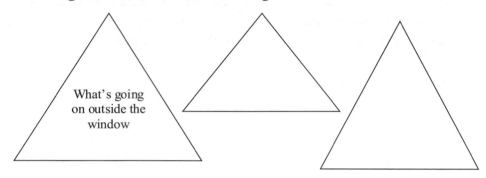

**HEARING things:**

**THINKING things:**

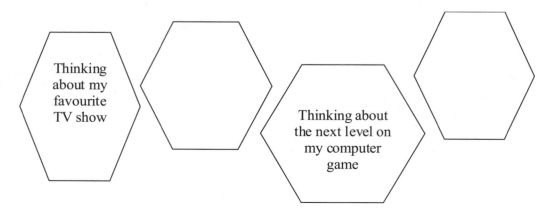

# Concentration Tricks: Survey

Everybody has problems concentrating from time to time and so most people learn tricks that help them to focus. In order to discover some of these tricks, complete the survey below by asking some adults, friends and classmates about what techniques they use. Zac has already started the survey for you.

| Name | Age | Fun fact about them | Concentration trick |
|------|-----|---------------------|---------------------|
| Zac | 14 | Can almost slam dunk the basketball | I play with a stress ball while I am reading |
|  |  |  |  |
|  |  |  |  |
|  |  |  |  |
|  |  |  |  |

# Tuning Back In: The Secret Code

Sometimes we lose concentration, and might need someone else to help us re-focus and tune back into the things we are supposed to be doing. When other people do this, they are trying to help us by making sure we get a chance to learn, join in, finish things and not fall behind. The hard part is to find a way for this to happen without it feeling like nagging or like you are in trouble!

Think about the ways that your teachers and your family try to draw your attention back when you have lost focus. What do they do? What do they say? Write some examples below:

_____

_____

You probably already have some good ideas on how your teachers and parents can help, so your CHALLENGE is this:

**Try to find a SECRET CODE that you can use together to help you re-focus, but that no-one else can know is being used!**

Listed below are some codes that other young people with ADHD have used. Tick any that you think might work for you, and add any others that you can come up with. Remember, they are things that the *adult* will do to help you re-focus.

☐   Walk past and tap on desk three times

☐   Ask you to run an errand

☐   Ask everyone to have a quick stretch

☐   Ask everyone to check their neighbour's work

☐   Clap hands and ask the whole class a question or check where they are up to

☐   Ask you an easy question (e.g. 'James, what lesson do you have next?')

☐   Give everyone a quick time check (e.g. 'OK everyone, it's 10.20, so 15 minutes to go')

☐   Look at your work and give you a compliment (e.g. 'Great, now you just need to…')

☐   _____

☐   _____

   

# Make a Fidget

Fidgets can be really handy! They help us by keeping our hands busy so that we can look, listen and focus better. They can also stop us from doing other 'fidgety' things that might annoy others or get us in trouble. The important thing is to find something *you* like to fidget with. So make these two ideas below and give them a try. See 'Top Tips' for more information.

| Stress balloons | Rate it |
|---|---|
| 1. Choose a balloon; place a funnel into the opening.<br><br>2. Spoon the fillings slowly into the funnel – try flour (soft and squishy), flour and uncooked rice (soft with interesting bits) and just rice (scrunchy).<br><br>3. Tie the balloon; push out as much air as possible.<br><br>4. If you tend to squeeze and pull things quite hard, try starting with one balloon inside another so you have a 'double layer' to prevent it bursting. | • Try it out: watching TV, in the car/bus, listening.<br><br>• Keep it in your pocket (let your teachers know).<br><br>• Make some for your friends and family.<br><br>☺ **Your score out of 10?**<br>\_\_\_\_ **/ 10** |

| Key chains | Rate it |
|---|---|
| 1. Find or buy a key-ring or karabiner (clip).<br><br>2. Choose some items to hang from this that you might like to fidget with: rubber bands, charity bracelet, keys, ornaments, stress balls.<br><br>3. Hook this to your belt loops or pencil case so it is always with you. | • Try to wear it so it is always handy.<br><br>• Try attaching something different every day.<br><br>☺ **Your score out of 10?**<br>\_\_\_\_ **/ 10** |

# Movement Breaks

Sometimes we need to give our brains some extra stimulation to keep ourselves focused. By moving our body and by working our muscles, we can help to keep our mind alert and organized. Some movements work better than others, so good tips to remember are: STEADY PACE, MAKE IT HARD and KEEP GOING. Try each of the exercises below and rate them. Try to keep practising these while you complete worksheets in other chapters!

## EXERCISES YOU CAN DO AT YOUR DESK

| Exercise | How to | Circle star rating: |
|---|---|---|
| Chair push-ups | Put hands on the sides of chair seat and push down so that you lift your bottom off the chair. Make sure your feet are off the floor! Do 10–20. | Fun: ☆ ☆ ☆ ☆ ☆<br>Effective: ☆ ☆ ☆ ☆ ☆ |
| Hand presses | Place palms together and press against each other as hard as you can. Hold for ten seconds, repeat five times. | Fun: ☆ ☆ ☆ ☆ ☆<br>Effective: ☆ ☆ ☆ ☆ ☆ |
| Head presses | First sit up straight. Link fingers together and place hands on top of head, then push down firmly. Hold for ten seconds, repeat five times. | Fun: ☆ ☆ ☆ ☆ ☆<br>Effective: ☆ ☆ ☆ ☆ ☆ |
| Sports water bottle | Have a drink from a water bottle with a sports top that takes a lot of effort to suck through. | Fun: ☆ ☆ ☆ ☆ ☆<br>Effective: ☆ ☆ ☆ ☆ ☆ |

## EXERCISES YOU CAN DO WITH A BIT OF SPACE

| Exercise | How to | Circle star rating: |
|---|---|---|
| Wall or floor push-up | Try push-ups standing against the wall or on the floor. Make sure your hands are under your shoulders and you bend/straighten your arms and keep your body still! Do 15–20. | Fun: ☆ ☆ ☆ ☆ ☆ <br> Effective: ☆ ☆ ☆ ☆ ☆ |
| Handstand against the wall | Start on your hands and knees and then 'walk' your feet up the wall behind you until your body is straight. Keep your feet leaning on the wall and hold for 15–20 seconds. | Fun: ☆ ☆ ☆ ☆ ☆ <br> Effective: ☆ ☆ ☆ ☆ ☆ |
| Table top | Sit on the floor, lean back and push your middle up so that your hands and feet are on the ground and your body and thighs are straight like a 'table top'. Hold for 20 seconds. | Fun: ☆ ☆ ☆ ☆ ☆ <br> Effective: ☆ ☆ ☆ ☆ ☆ |

## EXERCISES THAT ALSO 'HELP OUT'. CAN YOU THINK OF ANY OTHERS?

| | |
|---|---|
| Pushing/pulling heavy equipment (e.g. sports gear) | Walking with heavy backpack |
| Using a hand or foot pump to inflate balls/tyres | Crushing cans for recycling |
| Pushing lawn mower/wheelbarrow/vacuum | Digging in garden |
| Carrying heavy loads (e.g. book box) | Stacking/un-stacking chairs |

# Checklist Challenge

Checklists are a great way of keeping you focused on tasks that have a number of different steps. They also help you get organized, so there is a double bonus! You can even include your 'movement' breaks into your checklist. Here are two examples – have a good look at them. Can you see how the tasks have been broken up into steps?

| James's maths homework | Zac's library assignment |
|---|---|
| ☐ Clear desk – just maths stuff | ☐ Find a book on WWI |
| ☐ Fill up water bottle; keep handy | ☐ Find section on causes of war and take notes |
| ☐ Read textbook pg 100–103 (use fidget) | ☐ Find book on WWII |
| ☐ Worksheet Q 1–3 | ☐ Find section on causes of war and take notes |
| ☐ 10 chair push-ups | ☐ Compare – write down any causes that are the same and any causes that are different |
| ☐ Worksheet Q 4–5 | |
| ☐ Finish! | |

Now it is your turn to make a checklist. You have two things to decide, then give it a go!

1. Choose an activity to trial:

- A puzzle
- Some worksheets from this book
- A homework task
- 'Where's Wally'? activity

2. Choose checklist style:

- Notepad
- Small whiteboard
- Post-it notes; one step each, take off when done
- Clipboard/folder

**GOOD LUCK!**

# Exercise Planner

As you have probably figured out by now, the right kind of exercise can really help you to feel better, concentrate well and ultimately make school easier. Think about the sorts of exercise or activities you like to do. It could be anything from riding your bike, doing interactive computer games, jumping on the trampoline to doing push-ups. You might also want to look back at the 'Movement Breaks' worksheets for extra ideas. Fill out the exercise plan below with things you might be able to do every day.

| _____'s Exercise Plan | | |
|---|---|---|
| **Time of day** | **Activities** | **Time needed to do them** |
| Before school: | 1.<br><br>2. | |
| Between lessons/classes: | 1.<br><br>2. | |
| Lunch time: | 1.<br><br>2. | |
| Between lessons/classes: | 1.<br><br>2. | |
| After school: | 1.<br><br>2. | |

# What Could I Do If...?

Imagine yourself in the situations below and think about how you might respond using the ideas you have learnt from this chapter of the book. Make sure you read the 'Top Tips for Young People' first as they have some good ideas and hints!

**Situation 1:**
You have a geography test this afternoon and you want to do well so you need to make sure that you can concentrate. What could you do just before going into the test to help you focus?

_____

_____

_____

Where could you sit in the classroom to help you concentrate at your best?

_____

**Situation 2:**
You are sitting in class and your teacher is talking about an assignment you have due. Your mind is wandering off and you are struggling to listen to what is being said, but you really need to hear these tips. What could you do to help you focus?

_____

_____

What could your teacher do to help?

_____

_____

# Don't Miss A Thing!

Look back through the worksheets you have completed to help you answer the questions below.

**My concentration profile:**

Things I concentrate on well: _____

Times I find it hard to concentrate: _____

Things I get distracted by: _____

**My top three strategies to help me concentrate:**

1. _____

2. _____

3. _____

## WOULD CONCENTRATION BE A GOOD AREA TO WORK ON?

| | | | |
|---|---|---|---|
| Young person: | ☐ Yes | ☐ No | ☐ Maybe |
| Adult: | ☐ Yes | ☐ No | ☐ Maybe |

**If YES or MAYBE, see Chapter 9 for help with goal setting**

# Don't Miss A Thing! Take Control of Your Surroundings

When things around us distract us, the activities we are trying to do take longer. We don't do as good a job and sometimes things don't get finished. So taking control means getting rid of some of the distractions in our surroundings. This can be a bit hard at school (you might need to talk about these ideas with your teachers) but can definitely be done at home, in the library or during music lessons and sports training. Here are some tips for taking control by reducing different types of distractions.

### Reducing visual distractions:

- In class, go to the front so you don't look past lots of things that could distract you.
- At home, in the library or during group work, sit at a desk or chair that faces a wall rather than looking out into the room.
- Try sitting with your head leaning in your hand so you 'shield' your eyes from things happening and moving on that side.
- Keep your desk and nearby walls clear, with just the important things out for the task you are currently working on.

### Reducing auditory distractions:

Note: some people require *no* background noise to concentrate well, while others *need* constant and steady background noise (i.e. not too loud or with lots of changes).

- Turn off distracting and changing background noise such as TV, radio, etc.
- Try wearing headphones to block out noise. You can use the headphones without sound, or with quiet music, as long you don't catch yourself listening to it rather than focusing on your task!
- Avoid sitting next to people who talk all the time! It's hard if they are your friends but it might be better than missing them at lunch time because you are staying in to finish off your class work!

### Reducing thought distractions:

- If you think of something that you want to tell someone, and you are worried you will forget it, write down a few key words that will help you remember the thought later on.
- If you find that you are thinking about ALL the things you need to do, remind yourself that you can only do one thing at a time and decide on an order (step by step). You may want to write this down or put it in your diary.

> So what is the overall message?
>
> REDUCING DISTRACTIONS = BETTER CONCENTRATION

**Some other things that will help with concentration include:**

- getting organized
- avoid getting stressed
- keeping fit and healthy.

# Figuring Out Fidgets

Fidgets can be a great way to help keep you focused and get rid of some extra energy. The aim of using a fidget is to keep your hands busy so that you can look and listen well. They can also stop us from doing other 'fidgety' things that might annoy others or get us in trouble. Some good fidget tips are the following:

1.  **Find a fidget that works for you**. It could be:
    - squeezing (e.g. Blu-Tack, stress ball, bull-clip)
    - wrapping (e.g. pipe-cleaner/lace around finger)
    - stretching (e.g. charity bracelet, hair band)
    - feeling (e.g. textured ball, key-ring)
    - moving (e.g. doodling on separate pad, rolling a cord/shoelace).

2.  **Change your fidget regularly** so that you don't get bored with it.

3.  **Remember to use with care!** Making noise or lots of movements with your fidget is likely to annoy others – some people can be really sensitive to what they see and hear. Sometimes keeping fidgets out of sight rather than on the table might be best.

4.  **Make sure the fidget is always close by** and doesn't get lost or left behind. The best way of doing this is to attach it to you by clipping it to your belt loop. As a second option, you could attach it to your pencil case or bag.

5.  Remember that fidgets **can also help with stress** (as you will see in the 'Keeping Cool and Calm!' chapter).

# Don't Miss A Thing! Sensory Strategies

Sensory-based strategies are effective, practical and are one of the few ways in which we can temporarily increase the young person's capacity to concentrate. Remember that these strategies work for young people with either ADHD or ADD – you don't need to have hyperactivity to benefit from additional sensory input! It can be challenging to find ways to incorporate sensory strategies into structured environments such as the classroom. Whether you are contemplating the use of fidgets, movement breaks, exercise plans or any of the other ideas in this chapter (or recommended by other professionals), consider the following:

1.  Like anything new, *these strategies need to be learnt*, need to have boundaries and rules around them, and will initially need prompting and support for effective use. For example, young people will need to be reminded at first to use their fidgets, rather than picking up whatever is closest to hand.

2.  Strategies can be *introduced class wide* as they benefit everyone. Imagine that if during long meetings that *you* attended, everyone got to choose a fidget and stopped every 20 minutes to do two minutes of 'chair exercises'. Wouldn't your attention improve, and thereby your learning, participation and enjoyment?

3.  Remember that to have the most power and the greatest effect, these strategies need to be *done regularly, as part of day-to-day life, and be **intense***. Squeezing a stress ball is not going to be enough stimulation on its own – it might serve as a 'top up' during class but it needs to be part of an overall package of exercise and sensory input.

4.  Some people become concerned that by letting the young person have access to certain sensory strategies, *other students may view this as unfair*, or, alternatively, *that too much attention* might be drawn to the person. While these are very valid and natural concerns, consider these two points:

    (a)  These strategies are necessary 'tools' required to ensure that optimal learning can take place. We don't question whether a student with poor vision should wear glasses because of concerns that they might draw undue attention or identify the student as 'different'!

    (b)  Most other students are already *very* aware of the difficulties experienced by the young person with ADHD, especially if they are restless. These strategies will make sense to them! It is also OK to explain why these strategies are being used.

5.   As a young person moves into high school, the *use of strategies that appear more 'natural'* in this setting is of greater priority. Instead of fidgeting with a textured ball they might, for example, use a lump of Blu-Tack or a key-ring from a favourite sporting team. Regular 'jobs' such as helping set up the PE equipment or collecting messages could be arranged instead of classroom exercise breaks.

6.   As you will find out in later chapters of this book, these sensory strategies can also help with *stress management* – they help the brain to achieve a calm, yet alert, state.

# Don't Miss A Thing! Creating a Good 'Fit'

One of the most powerful concepts in working with any young person with attention difficulties is to create an environment in which they can perform to their best. We simply cannot expect them to work the same way as their peers! The good news is that with a bit of planning and preparation, we can make a huge difference. Some key adjustments are the following:

1. **Reduce surrounding distractions** by adopting techniques such as:

   - positioning the young person at the front of the class and away from windows
   - completing work at individual workstations rather than group tables (e.g. in the library)
   - encouraging everyone to put away unnecessary equipment/books
   - keeping boards and classrooms clean/clear so relevant information stands out.

2. **Break up activities** into smaller, readily achievable steps with mini-breaks in between. Ensure each step has a definite end point using time (e.g. 15 minutes) and/or a set amount of work (e.g. five questions) as the determiner.

3. **Add 'doing' elements** to tasks where possible (e.g. measure, build, draw, underline). Vary working positions between sitting, standing, floor work and walking/moving.

4. **Give clear instructions** using strategies such as:

   - getting attention first (e.g. clap, call names: 'Everyone…Tom, Leah, Claire…')
   - giving information step by step using simple short sentences and backing this up with written/visual information (e.g. list on board, worksheet, demonstrate)
   - having the individual and the group repeat the steps back to you or to each other
   - remembering not to rely on where the young person is looking as an indicator of attention (eye contact helps but doesn't always equal attention).

5. **Use technology** such as PowerPoint, interactive software and laser pointers.

# Don't Miss A Thing!

## BOOKS

- *Learning to Slow Down and Pay Attention* by Kathleen Nadeau and Ellen Dixon, 2004, American Psychological Corporation.
- *Fidget to Focus. Outwit Your Boredom: Sensory Strategies for Living with ADD* by Roland Rotz and Sarah Wright, 2005, iUniverse (www.fidgettofocus.com/index.html).
- *SI Tools for Teens: Strategies to Promote Sensory Processing Handbook* by Diana Henry *et al.*, 2004, Henry OT Services.
- *Helping Hyperactive Kids – A Sensory Integration Approach* by Lynn Horowitz and Cecile Rost, 2007, Hunter House.

## INTERNET SITES

- ADHD Directory: www.addconsults.com/articles/full.php3?id=1488
- The Alert Program: www.alertprogram.com

# CHAPTER 5

# Keeping Cool and Calm!

People of all ages and backgrounds experience stress. However, what makes each of us feel stressed, and how we respond, varies greatly. Stress can have a significant effect on us, altering our mood, behaviour, thinking and physical state (e.g. breathing, heart rate). Indeed, feeling stressed too often can lead to problems across multiple facets of our lives.

Stress is often manifested in different ways at different ages. So what does it look like in young people? Typically, they demonstrate stress through their behaviour; they may be prone to crying more, develop sleep problems, act like a younger child, withdraw into themselves or argue a lot with those around them. Their mood may become more irritable, angry, worried or simply unhappy.

It can be difficult to determine when a young person's thinking is being affected by stress, as they often find it hard to express their thoughts. You might notice that they are more likely to think negatively if they are stressed, frequently expecting the worst to happen. Cognitive skills such as concentration, memory and planning are also typically affected.

As our bodies play a key role in the stress response, physical changes can also be possible indicators. There are short-term reactions such as changes to skin colour, muscle tension and breathing. There may also be wider physical changes linked with prolonged stress. You could observe indicators such as a poor immune system, an increase or decrease in appetite, sleep difficulties and an increase in restlessness (e.g. fidgety behaviour).

## ADHD AND STRESS

Young people with ADHD can have a lot to feel stressed about! For example, they might do things they regret due to their impulsivity, they might find it difficult to finish tasks due to their inattention and they might find themselves getting in trouble for fidgeting due to their restlessness. Any one of these scenarios could trigger negative emotional responses, particularly when they happen on a regular basis.

In addition, young people with ADHD often struggle to manage their stress effectively. For example, they might find it difficult to monitor their feelings and detect the early signs of stress. They may overreact to situations and emotions, and switch into 'fight and flight' responses. They may also find it difficult to effectively calm themselves down, particularly by using words and talking strategies. Feelings of worry, frustration and being misunderstood can sometimes lead to aggressive or avoidant behaviour if not managed effectively. There is no surprise that this will subsequently have a negative impact on many aspects of their life, such as friendships, school participation, family relationships and extra-curricular activities.

## CHALLENGES AT HIGH SCHOOL

As young people with ADHD make the transition to high school they will be confronted with many more stress triggers, for example friendship changes, increased demands from teachers and multiple deadlines to meet. In addition there will be an increase in expectations, particularly with regard to punctuality, learning, organization and behaviour. At high school there is often significantly less support available from staff and the emphasis is on individuals managing stressful situations independently.

## OBJECTIVES

Whether we are aware of it or not, we have all learnt and adopted strategies to help us manage our stress. Some strategies are more effective than others, and some are hard to recognize until we sit down and think about them. Young people with ADHD need to develop strategies that are 'powerful' enough to manage their increased experience of stress. They need strategies that are readily accessible and they need help to build these into day-to-day life in order to help prevent and minimize the stress response.

The worksheets and tip sheets in this chapter are designed to support the following processes:

- To help the young person understand that everyone experiences stress, and that we all need to learn to manage stress.

- To help the young person to learn about their own stress – what their triggers are, how their body responds and how their behaviour changes.

- To help you and the young person identify and try out strategies that are effective in reducing stress at an early stage and to start practising these in everyday situations.

Some of the strategies recommended in this chapter work by changing the young person's thoughts and focus. However, most work towards changing their physical state. By using physical and sensory means, we directly 'calm' and 'relax' our physical responses and internal state, and as a result change how we are feeling. There is considerable evidence to support this approach, and if you are interested in more information on how this works please refer to the resources list at the end of the chapter.

# Stress Volcano

Stress can be like a volcano – when you feel calm there is no smoke or lava, and then when you start to 'rumble' (get annoyed or wound up), smoke starts to appear and the lava is bubbling inside. When you 'explode' the volcano erupts with smoke, lava and rocks that go everywhere! Next to the three pictures below, write about what happens when you get stressed – **what your body does, how you feel and how you act**. Zac has started this worksheet to help you out, so highlight his points if they apply to you, and underneath add your own.

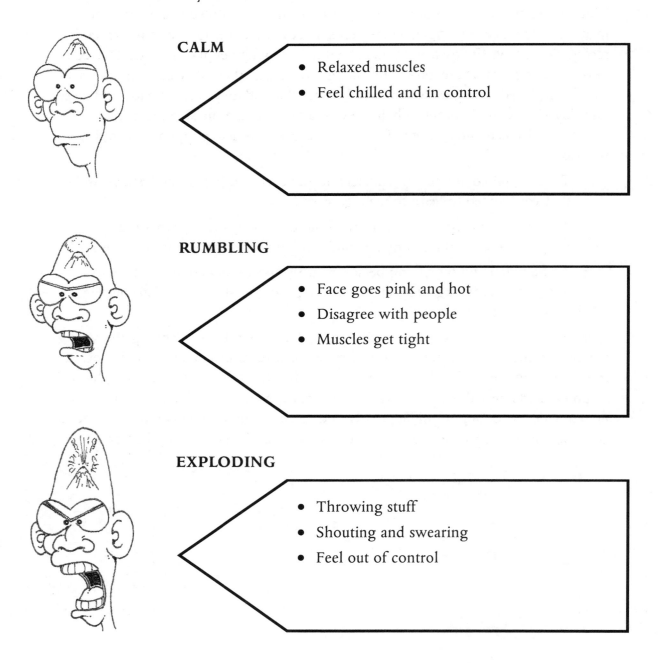

**CALM**

- Relaxed muscles
- Feel chilled and in control

**RUMBLING**

- Face goes pink and hot
- Disagree with people
- Muscles get tight

**EXPLODING**

- Throwing stuff
- Shouting and swearing
- Feel out of control

# When I Get Stressed I...

You have already started thinking about the things you might do at different stages of feeling 'stressed'. Some of these things might be in the table below – place a tick next to each one that you do, and a cross for the ones you don't. Are there any other ways that you react in a stressful situation? Add them to the list as well.

Once you have finished filling in the sheet about yourself, try to 'interview' two other people (friends or family) and see how they respond when they get stressed.

| When I get stressed I... | Me: (✓ or X) | Name: (✓ or X) | Name: (✓ or X) |
|---|---|---|---|
| Shout | | | |
| Walk away | | | |
| Hang out in my room | | | |
| Talk over the top of people | | | |
| Listen to music | | | |
| Give up trying | | | |
| Hit or push | | | |
| Say things I regret | | | |
| Ignore people | | | |
| Bite my nails/pick at things | | | |
| | | | |
| | | | |
| | | | |

Do you think your responses to stress are helpful? Discuss your thoughts on this.

# Triggers of Stress

Think about what makes you feel stressed at home and at school. Here are a few things that Zac, Carly and James find stressful. Shade in or highlight the ones that fit for you and add some of your own ideas in the blank circles.

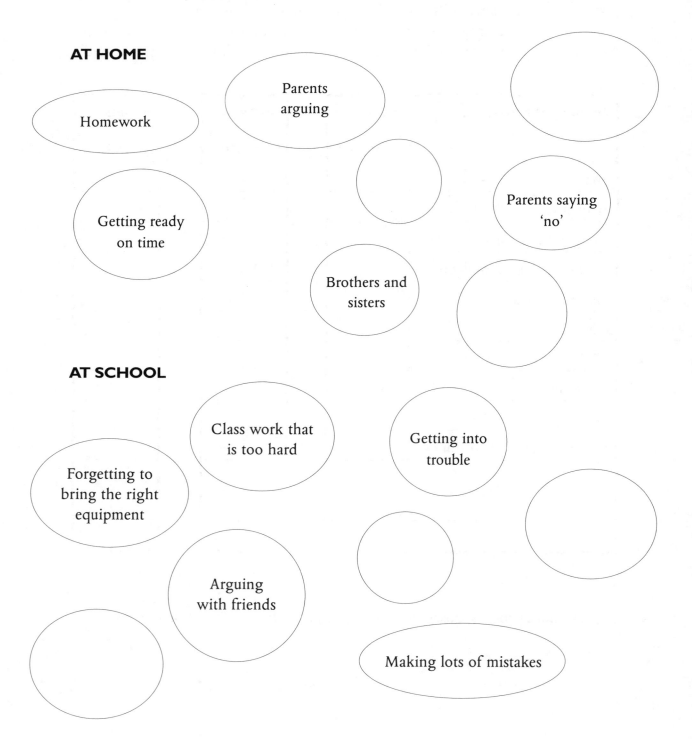

**AT HOME**

Homework

Parents arguing

Getting ready on time

Parents saying 'no'

Brothers and sisters

**AT SCHOOL**

Class work that is too hard

Getting into trouble

Forgetting to bring the right equipment

Arguing with friends

Making lots of mistakes

# What Helps to Calm Me Down?

Whether we realize it or not, we all use strategies to help us calm down in times of stress. Look through the examples we have put together. If you have used any of these techniques and they have helped, highlight the words in coloured pen. Add any extra ideas about what has helped you to chill out into the 'thought bubble'.

| | |
|---|---|
| Reading | Having a bath or shower |
| Going somewhere quiet | Talking it through |
| Listening to music | Singing or whistling |
| Going for a walk | Playing with a pet |
| Exercise or playing sports | Laughing |

Find two people and interview them about the things that help them calm down when they are stressed. Get them to write their answers here:

| Name: | Name: |
|---|---|
| • | • |
| • | • |
| • | • |

# Relaxation

Relaxation is a really popular way of staying calm and in control. It works by helping you to relax the stressed-out muscles in your body AND helps you to tackle the stressful thoughts in your head. Lots of people use relaxation techniques, including top sportspeople and musicians. Here are two types of relaxation styles for you to try – tense and relax and visualization. Before you get started, read through the important tips below.

## TIPS FOR RELAXATION

- Practise! The first few times you try relaxation exercises you may not feel very relaxed as you will be trying to concentrate on the instructions. So it is important that you practise relaxation regularly, just like learning to ride a bike or play football. The more you practise, the easier the relaxation will be and the more relaxed you will feel.

- It might be useful to try relaxation with one or two other people for the first few times. Once you get the hang of it you can even start to teach others!

- The instructions can be read out by someone or you could record them onto a tape and play it back. The person will need to speak in a calm, slow voice with pauses between sentences.

- It is important to set up the room you are relaxing in to help you chill out. Try to choose a room that is quiet and private so that other people won't distract you. If you can, allow yourself about 20 minutes to do the exercises.

# Tense and Relax Exercise

## STEP 1: GET IN POSITION

Lie down on your back or sit somewhere comfortable and keep your eyes closed as you do the activity.

## STEP 2: TENSE AND RELAX THE DIFFERENT BODY PARTS

1. **Hands and arms**

   Make a fist with your right hand; squeeze it hard. Feel the tightness in your hand and arm as you squeeze. Now let your hand go and relax. Notice the difference between your hand when it is tense and relaxed. Once again make a fist with your right hand and squeeze. Well done. Now relax and let your hand go. Repeat this for your left hand and arm.

2. **Arms and shoulders**

   Now stretch your arms out above your head, feel the pull in your shoulders as you stretch further – stretch as far as you can. Drop your arms back by your side. Now stretch again, raise your arms above your head and let them drop quickly. Well done. Notice how your shoulders feel more relaxed. Again stretch your arms up above your head and reach high above you, feel the tension in your arms and shoulders. Let them drop quickly and feel how good it is to be relaxed. Great.

TENSE                    RELAX

**97**

3.   **Shoulders**

Let's work your shoulders. Pull them up to your ears and make your neck disappear. Hold it tight and then relax. Again pull your shoulders up to your ears and push your head down into your shoulders. Hold it and then relax your shoulders. Notice how relaxed your shoulders and neck feel. Let's do it one more time; push your shoulders up high to your ears. Hold it. Now relax your shoulders. Good work.

4.   **Face**

Wrinkle up your nose and the rest of your face. Notice that your forehead and mouth get tight too. Hold it tight. Now relax your nose and face. Let's do it again; wrinkle up your nose. Hold it as tight as you can. Good. Relax your face now; feel your whole face relax. Now wrinkle up your forehead by raising your eyebrows. Hold it and then let it go so your face is smooth. Well done.

5.   **Stomach**

Now tighten up your stomach muscles and make your stomach really hard. Pull your belly button in towards your spine and hold it tight. Then relax your stomach so it goes soft. Notice that it feels different. Let's do it again.

6.   **Chest**

Breathe deeply in through your nose and out through your mouth. Breathe in again and feel your chest and ribs move out, hold, and then breathe out and let your chest and ribs collapse. Let's do it two more times – in, hold, and then out; in, hold, and then out.

## STEP 3: REST AND ENJOY!

Stay still for a few minutes and enjoy the feeling of warmth and heaviness in your body.

# Relax on Chill-Out Beach

Find somewhere comfortable to lie down. The person reading this needs to read slowly and pause between each sentence – aim for it to take at least five minutes!

Close your eyes, be very still and imagine you are lying on a sunny beach, with golden sand. The beautiful calm sea is lapping against the shore. You can see colourful flowers and tall palm trees along the beach. The trees are blowing gently in the breeze. You can feel the warm sand beneath your feet and body.

The warm sun is on your face and a lovely breeze keeps you cool. You can hear the waves coming and going and the palm trees blowing in the wind. You can smell the exotic flowers. You feel relaxed and calm in your body and in your mind.

Slowly breathe out and say 'relax' in your head each time you breathe out. You can still feel the warm sand beneath you. Your breathing is calm and relaxed. Listen to the sea. The warm water is lapping at your toes. You can feel the water warm on your body, on your legs, arms and back. You are floating on the water and your body feels relaxed as it gently bobs up and down, up and down.

Now that you are completely relaxed, the warm water starts slowly moving away. As the water goes, little by little, it takes away your worries. The water moves past your head, your chest, your stomach, your legs, and then your feet. Now you can again feel the soft warm sand under your body. You can feel the sun warming you and smell the salt drying. You feel calm, relaxed and peaceful.

And now, when you are ready to, slowly wake up from the Chill-Out Beach. Take a deep breath, wiggle your fingers and toes, have a big stretch and open your eyes.

# Stress Busters

Try each of these exercises and rate whether they could help you to manage your stress while it is still at the 'rumbling' stage. Are they good (thumbs up), OK (thumb sideways) or not for you (thumbs down)? It is good to end up with a number of different stress busters so you can choose one that suits where you are (home, school, football club, etc.) and what mood you are in. It may take a while to get the equipment together so you might want to spread this exercise over a few sessions.

## MAKE THOSE MUSCLES WORK!

| | | | |
|---|---|---|---|
| **Slurp and suck**: Have a drink from a sports water bottle or drink from a glass using a straw. | 👎 | 👉 | 👍 |
| **Push-ups**: Try these on the floor, against the wall, on the chair (push down on seat and lift up bottom). Keep going until you can't do any more! | 👎 | 👉 | 👍 |
| **Blowing**: Take a deep breath and then put something to your lips so that you have to blow hard to get the air around it. You could use a pen or your finger. Repeat 5–10 times. | 👎 | 👉 | 👍 |
| **Push, pull or squeeze**: Push using a foot or hand pump, 'rowing' exercises using an elastic yoga band, squeeze a large ball of Blu-Tack/plasticine/theraputty | 👎 | 👉 | 👍 |
| **Chew, crunch or suck on food** – gum, raisins, bagels, pretzels, carrots. Suck on hard sweets (try sugarless). | 👎 | 👉 | 👍 |

## TOUCHY FEELY!

| | | | |
|---|---|---|---|
| **Fidget** with different objects. Try:<br>• squeezing (e.g. Blu-Tack, stress ball, bull-clip)<br>• wrapping (e.g. pipe-cleaner/lace around finger)<br>• stretching (e.g. charity bracelet, hair band)<br>• feeling (e.g. textured ball, key-ring) | 👎 | 👉 | 👍 |
| **Vibration**: Use a vibrating massager or cushion on your arms/body. (Warning: some people don't like this feeling so maybe try an electric toothbrush as a test.) | 👎 | 👉 | 👍 |
| **Get comfy**: Try different positions that give your body lots of calming touch: lie on your back or tummy on the floor, sit in a beanbag/armchair, and have cushions to use as well. Try combining this with other strategies. | 👎 | 👉 | 👍 |
| **Hand massage**: Use your thumb to massage the palm of your other hand. Press firmly. Gradually work up each finger in long strokes, and then change hands. | 👎 | 👉 | 👍 |

## HAVE A LAUGH!

| | | | |
|---|---|---|---|
| **Movie scene**: Find one of your favourite funny scenes in a movie and memorize it so that you can 'play' it in your head and make yourself chuckle. | 👎 | 👉 | 👍 |
| **Joke of the day**: Write down a few jokes that make you laugh or find some funny pictures. | 👎 | 👉 | 👍 |

## SOUND AND LIGHT SHOW!

| | | | |
|---|---|---|---|
| **Separate space**: Find a space without too many things to look at – the corner of a room, lying down looking at the ceiling, etc. Try combining this with music and/or a fidget. | 👎 | ✊ | 👍 |
| **Music**: Listen to music that you find relaxing and that has a steady beat and melody. You may want to try some specific relaxation music. Consider using earphones to block out the background noise. Some people like just earphones without the music! | 👎 | ✊ | 👍 |
| **Images**: Look at something calming such as fish in an aquarium, lava lamp, glitter wands, fibre optic lights, a slinky or a video of fire/waves. | 👎 | ✊ | 👍 |

# Create a Chill-Out Space

Chill-out spaces are calm, safe and comfortable areas that help you relax and re-focus. They are places to go when you feel those *first* signs of stress (rumbling) in order to help stop the 'volcano' from erupting. Chill-out spaces can be made anywhere, including school, but for this activity you are going to make one at home.

**What you need to do is:**

1. Fill out the table on the next page so you have a PLAN of what you think you can do – remember you need to use things you already have at home.

2. Show this to your parents or carers. Check if your plan could work or together come up with some alternatives. Go through the 'Tips' (below) and agree on some instructions about how you will use the space.

3. Try it for a week at home and then fill in the 'report card' at the end.

**Tips:**

- Avoid putting games into the space – it isn't a second bedroom!
- You should never be forced to use the chill-out area. It isn't a punishment or 'time out' space.
- You can choose to go there whenever you want, but you may need to set a rough time limit.
- Organize agreed ways in which your parents/carers can suggest that it might be helpful to use the space (e.g. 'How about five minutes to chill out?' or use a signal like the 'OK' sign).
- Add any extra family rules you might need.

# Plan for Creating a Chill-Out Space

| Step | What I need to do | Plan | Tick when done |
|------|-------------------|------|----------------|
| **Where** | Choose a space away from busy areas (e.g. corner of room, hallway, spare room) | | |
| **Privacy** | Screen your space as much as possible, e.g. using furniture, away from windows/TVs | | |
| **Comfy** | Wrap your body up using beanbags, cushions, heavy blankets, armchairs | | |
| **Stress busters** | Add a few of the things you liked from the 'Stress Busters' activity – no more than three | | |
| **Relaxation** | Have a sheet on the wall or tape/CD with a relaxation activity you enjoyed | | |
| **Who** | Decide if this space is just for you or if anyone in the family can use it | | |

# Report Card For Chill-Out Space

*From the International Institute of Chill-Out Spaces Ltd*

**REPORT CARD for** _____ **FAMILY**

**Date:** _____

1.  Did the chill-out space get set up?                           Yes/No

2.  How many times was the chill-out space used?      _____ in the week

3.  Overall rating for the family having 'Given It A Go'?   A / B / C / D

4.  Did you like spending time in the chill-out space?      Yes / No / Sometimes

5.  Did you find it relaxing?                                        Yes / No / Sometimes

6.  Overall rating for the space and 'How well it worked'?   A / B / C / D

Comments and suggestions from the evaluator:

Comments and suggestions from family members:

Signature of evaluator: _____

Name of evaluator: _____

# Doing Things Differently

Think about a situation that happened recently – one that ended up with you getting stressed. Ask an adult for some ideas if you are struggling to remember something. Fill out the boxes below, thinking about what DID happen and then what COULD have happened if you had done things differently.

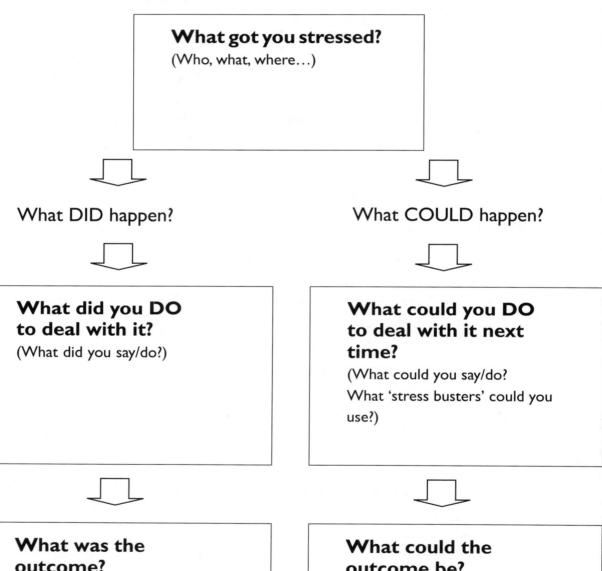

**What got you stressed?**
(Who, what, where…)

What DID happen?

What COULD happen?

**What did you DO to deal with it?**
(What did you say/do?)

**What could you DO to deal with it next time?**
(What could you say/do? What 'stress busters' could you use?)

**What was the outcome?**
(How did it end up? Good and bad points?)

**What could the outcome be?**
(How could it end up? Good and bad points?)

# What Could I Do If…?

Imagine yourself in the situations below, and think about how you might respond using the ideas you have learnt from this chapter of the book.

**Situation 1:**
You have been out playing on the sports fields with your friends during break and are feeling really wound up and excited. You have to go back into the classroom – what can you do to help yourself calm down so that you can sit well and do your work?

_____

_____

_____

**Situation 2:**
Your brother/sister is being really annoying and you can feel yourself getting fed up with them and becoming more and more stressed. What can you do?

_____

_____

_____

# Keeping Cool and Calm!

Look back through the worksheets you have completed to help answer the questions below.

**How do I know when I am starting to get stressed?**

What my body does: _____

How I feel (emotions): _____

How I act: _____

**My top three strategies to chill out:**

1. _____

2. _____

3. _____

### WOULD KEEPING COOL AND CALM BE A GOOD AREA TO WORK ON?

| | | | |
|---|---|---|---|
| Young person: | ☐ Yes | ☐ No | ☐ Maybe |
| Adult: | ☐ Yes | ☐ No | ☐ Maybe |

**If YES or MAYBE, see Chapter 9 for help with goal setting**

# Keeping Cool and Calm!

There are lots of strategies in this chapter that help you figure out how to deal with stress in a positive way. These are really important and can make a huge difference in your life and in your friendships, both at home and at school.

It is also good to think about the day-to-day things that will help you manage your stress levels. By trying to lead a balanced and fun lifestyle, you can actually help to PREVENT a lot of stress and the problems that come with it. Some of our top tips are:

1. **Get active!** Regular exercise is great for releasing tension and gives you a 'happy buzz' (lots of natural chemicals are released that make you feel good). Getting active might be playing sport, going to the local park, walking the dog, riding your bike, dancing in your room or doing some push-ups and crunches.

2. **Give yourself time.** Rushing is nearly always stressful, and sometimes even leads to arguments and problems later on (e.g. when you realize you have forgotten something!). Making sure you give yourself enough time to get ready for things is vital. It is also good to have 'chill-out' times in between events so you avoid having to rush from one thing to another.

3. **Have a laugh.** It is almost impossible to feel stressed while you are having a good laugh or sharing a joke. So make time to have some fun each day!

4. **Sleep.** Without the right amount of sleep, our body and brain does not work as effectively and we often become grumpy and irritable. How do you respond to lack of sleep? Most people find they get more stressed when they are tired. It is great to develop a routine with your sleep, so that you go to bed and wake up at roughly the same time every day.

5. **Healthy eating.** Try to eat a balanced diet every day with plenty of fruit, vegetables, meat and grains (e.g. bread, rice and pasta). Drink plenty of water as well. When our body and brain get the nutrients they need, we can cope better with stress.

6. **Using tips from the other chapters** will also help your stress levels. Feeling good about yourself, having fun with friends, getting organized, reducing the hassle involved with completing homework and managing your fidgeting will all help to make life as 'stress-less' as possible.

7. **Working it out.** Remember that stress is natural and something that everyone goes through. What causes us stress will change with time and place. So talk about it with your family, your friends or any other important people in your life. They might have great tips and ideas that have worked for them, and they might learn something from you as well!

# Keeping Cool and Calm!

Here are our top tips on simple ways that you can help young people to manage their stress in everyday situations:

- **Timing is everything.** It is vital to remember that strategies should only be used at the early 'rumbling' stages of stress. Once the young person is 'exploding' no strategy will be effective, and time and space are typically the only appropriate responses. Using strategies at this time can be problematic – adults give up on good strategies as they seem ineffective and young people come to dislike the techniques because they link them to being upset/angry.

- **Lead by example.** Spend some time thinking about your own responses to stress. Often we could all do with improving our skills in handling stress – it could be a good idea to practise some of the strategies in this book alongside the young person! The more that you are in control of your own stress, the more able you are to support others. It is also helpful for young people to realize that learning and refining these skills is something that we all need to do.

- **Stay calm.** Any signs of anxiety or frustration shown by you will only increase the young person's stress levels. Check your voice and body language and practise 'faking it'!

- **Learn the 'warning signs'.** Identify the early signs of stress that are unique to the young person (the 'rumbling' stage). Doing something at this point in order to prevent the build up of stress is much easier than dealing with the 'explosion'.

- **Don't add demands.** When you detect early signs of stress, make sure you do not add extra demands on the young person or remind them of all the things they should and/or need to be doing. Instead use some of the strategies in the book as a form of short break OR give them space OR actually reduce the demands (e.g. 'let's finish this one and then come back to it some other time'). Remember that the priority is to avoid escalation.

- **Use humour and be playful.** This helps to quickly change the mood, gives the young person a 'breathing space' in which they may be able to regain control and ensures that feelings of shame and blame do not emerge and further escalate the situation.

# Challenging Behaviours

Understanding and managing problematic behaviour is a complex topic and needs to be addressed on a very individual basis. Suggested readings on this topic are included under the 'Resources' section; however, some general considerations include:

- Young people with ADHD have **reduced skills and abilities** when it comes to curbing impulses, regulating their responses, thinking through and problem solving. As a result they will always struggle to manage their behaviours even when they know the rules and care about the consequences. Therefore any behaviour management system will need to be **flexible**, and include strategies such as warning systems, options for withdrawal and tolerance of low-level behaviours.

- **Look beyond the behaviour** and try to respond to the message underneath, such as 'I can't cope', 'I don't know what to do' or 'I am feeling embarrassed'. What is the purpose of the behaviour? What function does it serve for the young person? This will be the key to determining the most effective response.

- Be mindful that **if you stop or limit a specific behaviour** without addressing the underlying purpose, other equally as challenging behaviours are likely to emerge. The need will still have to be met.

- **Positive behaviour systems** will be more effective than punishment-driven systems and will also avoid any negative impact on the young person's self-esteem. Positive strategies include working towards incentives, opportunities to express and demonstrate strengths and rewarding the efforts that have been made.

- Young people with ADHD are **socially vulnerable**, no matter how 'tough' they act. They are particularly susceptible to imitating negative role models in order to fit in, and to being targeted by others as the 'fall guy'. Be mindful of this and the increased social pressure they are under in order to feel accepted.

- Key strategies for **long-term prevention and management** of problem behaviours include:

  - **Adjusting the environment and programme**: Make modifications by reducing distractions, breaking tasks into small steps, setting realistic targets, creating an effective support structure and developing a regular routine.

  - **Teaching skills**: Develop competencies in areas such as stress management, conflict resolutions, social skills, communication skills and study skills.

○ **Preventing escalation**: Deal with early signs of stress in a way that is calming and prevents escalation (e.g. short breaks, discussion away from an audience, not forcing decisions/replies, changing topics, avoiding arguments).

○ **Be prepared**: Expect fluctuations in how the young person can deal with things. Remember that their reactions will vary from day to day and situation to situation. Also be aware that strategies will change in their effectiveness – always have a few up your sleeve! Problem solving and flexibility are essential.

• **When a young person 'explodes'** and their stress makes them unable to control their actions remember that there is nothing you can do apart from giving them the space and time to calm down. Make sure you don't rush in with requests, advice or reflection too soon afterwards, as the stress may flare up again. They need a significant period of 'recovery' time.

• Try to think about how to manage the young person's stress as part of their **overall lifestyle**. How can you build in opportunities for regular exercise? Can you think of typical times or activities that trigger stress (e.g. homework, getting ready in the morning)? How can you reduce the difficulties experienced at these times?

# Keeping Cool and Calm!

## SENSORY STRATEGIES

- The Alert Program: www.alertprogram.com
- Sensory Connection Program: www.sensoryconnectionprogram.com
- *Helping Hyperactive Kids – A Sensory Integration Approach* by Lynn Horowitz and Cecile Rost, 2007, Hunter House Publishers.

## RELAXATION

- Relax Kids: www.relaxkids.co.uk
- *Relaxation for Children* by Jenny Rickard, 1994, The Australian Council for Education Research Ltd.
- Yoga Kit for Kids: www.amazon.com

## STRESS MANAGEMENT

- *A Volcano in My Tummy: Helping Children to Handle Anger* by E. Whitehouse and W. Pudney, 1997, New Society Publishers.
- *Cool Cats, Calm Kids: Relaxation and Stress Management for Young People* by M. Williams and D. O'Quinn Burke, 1996, Impact Publishers.
- *Be the Boss of Your Stress: Self-Care for Kids* by Timothy Culbert, MD and Rebecca Kajander, 2007, Free Spirit Publishing Inc.
- *Hot Stones and Funny Bones: Teens Helping Teens Cope with Stress and Anger* by Brian Luke Seaward and Linda K. Bartlett, 2002, Health Communications Inc.
- *Think Good Feel Good: A Cognitive Behaviour Therapy Workbook for Children and Young People* by Paul Stallard, 2002, Wiley Blackwell.

## BEHAVIOUR MANAGEMENT

- *Can't Learn, Won't Learn, Don't Care: Trouble-Shooting Challenging Behaviour* by Fintan O'Regan, 2007, Continuum International Publishing.
- *The Source for ADD/ADHD* by Gail J. Richard and Joy L. Russell, 2001, Lingui Systems.

# Getting Sorted: Organization

We often talk about organization skills, but what does it actually take to be organized? The most accurate answer is that it takes: 'Lots of skills, and some that are quite advanced!' For example, to plan ahead you need to have a good memory, be able to hold lots of different bits of information in your mind at the one time, process/manipulate them at the same time, determine possible outcomes by projecting into the future and then make decisions based on all this information. To be organized, you need to be able to break tasks into steps, put them in order, and then adjust this plan as changes or problems arise. Organization also demands that an individual takes responsibility and control over an activity or group of tasks. No wonder that organization is an ongoing challenge for most of us!

It is also important to acknowledge that there is no one 'right' way of being organized. Instead, it is important that people find a style and a system that suits them – their learning style, their personality, their environment and their lifestyle. The way one person wants to organize their cupboards, get their house cleaned, meet deadlines and catch up with friends is often very different to another person's! Working under someone else's system can be very challenging. Organization is not about being 'tidy, neat and clean all the time' or living like a 'robot to a set schedule'. It is about putting your own personal system in place so that you get the boring stuff done with minimal time and stress, leaving plenty of time to do the things you love.

## ADHD AND ORGANIZATION

Difficulties with organization are one of the most frequently identified problems for young people with ADHD.

This is due in part to the difficulties they experience with:

- attention (e.g. don't get information 'in' and therefore don't remember)
- impulsivity (e.g. can't stick to a course, always go off on tangent, act without thinking things through, jump to conclusions)
- learning/processing styles (e.g. orientated to 'doing' rather than 'thinking through', difficulties processing more than one piece of information, difficulties with auditory information, poor comprehension of time).

There is some great information available on 'executive dysfunction' and ADHD, which details many of the areas of specific learning difficulties linked to this condition. If you are interested in learning more about this, there are recommended resources at the end of this chapter. In practice you will observe that young people with ADHD have difficulties with organization across many different areas of skill, including problems:

- organizing possessions (e.g. having the right equipment, finding things)
- organizing thoughts (e.g. starting a conversation at the beginning, putting steps in the right order, seeing the big picture plus the details)

**115**

- organizing learning (e.g. formatting work on the page, answering all the questions, checking answers/responses, adjusting work based on feedback)
- organizing actions (e.g. only using necessary movements, preparing/positioning before starting, monitoring own performance).

## CHALLENGES AT HIGH SCHOOL

At primary/elementary school, children with ADHD can often rely on their family and their teachers to help them get organized. The days are highly structured with clear instructions and allocated time to help organize the right response (e.g. what equipment to bring, what homework to do on what nights). Some young people also receive additional support in the form of teaching assistants or modified programmes. It is easy for a young person with ADHD to depend on these supports, rather than learning the skills needed for the expected levels of independence in high school. With the loss of this support, difficulties with organization can quickly lead to a cycle of failure, high levels of conflict both at home and school, loss of independence and difficulties in participating and socializing.

## OBJECTIVES

The general principles for supporting organization skills are similar to all those outlined throughout the book – meeting the young person half way. While supporting them in developing new skills is essential, so too is adjusting expectations and putting in routines and systems to ensure there is additional support for their very real difficulties.

The worksheets and advice sheets in this chapter are designed to support the following processes:

1.  To help the young person to learn about the importance of organization and reflect on their own organizational skills.

2.  To create an opportunity to explore and test new strategies that might help the young person develop their own systems for organization.

3.  To help identify strategies that work and to start practising them in day-to-day situations.

# What is Organization?

Essentially, to be organized is to have a SYSTEM. A system helps us to know where things are, get things done quickly, remember things, get to places on time and have all the things with us that we need. Without organization, life is chaos!

Take a DVD, for example. When you put it on it doesn't start playing half-way through. It always starts at the menu, and is ORGANIZED so that you know where to find things – the movie, the extras and the interviews. It even breaks the movie up into different sections so you can find just what you want. Can you imagine how frustrating it would be without this, or if all DVDs used a different system?

Colour in or highlight the things that you think are linked to being **well organized**. There should be a simple pattern at the end! You can check your answers using the answer sheet in 'Top Tips for Young People' at the end of this chapter.

| | | | | |
|---|---|---|---|---|
| Having a system | Being boring | Never finding things | Forgetting things | Making time for fun |
| Knowing where stuff is | Having a place for things | Leaving things at home | Making things simple | Knowing what comes next |
| Using a schedule/diary | Not getting things finished | Having a plan | Being late | Thinking about the future |
| Having a routine | Getting to places on time | Just seeing what happens | Places to start and stop | Having the things you need |
| Making things stress free | Being a nerd | Starting wherever | Losing things | Breaking things into steps |

# Organization Of The Rich and Famous!

Write down the name of your favourite sports star: _____

(If you are not into sport choose your favourite singer/band.)

What things would they need to do each day (e.g. practice, meetings, TV shows, eating meals, autographs)?

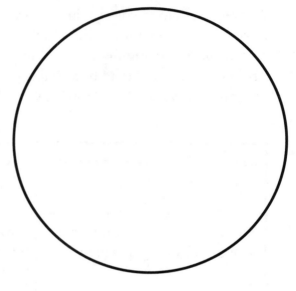

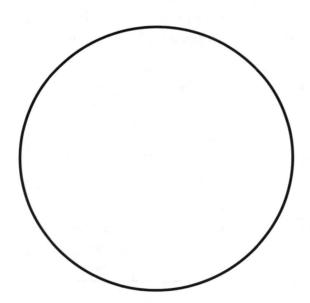

What would happen if they were late to these things, forgot to turn up or brought the wrong stuff with them?

Do you think they need to be ORGANIZED? _____

# Organization Survey

We asked Zac and Carly what they do to get organized and the good things that happen as a result. Now it is your turn – interview **three people** you know and find out what works for them. Put their answers into the table below.

| Name | Things they do to help get organized | How it makes them feel | What good things happen as a result |
|---|---|---|---|
| Zac | Has a different drawer for each type of clothes (socks, shorts, shirts) | Cool, calm and collected | Knows where stuff is so is quicker getting ready and has more time to sleep in! |
| Carly | Has a 'reminders list' on a whiteboard in her bedroom | Happy, as her Mum isn't always nagging her! | Remembers what she needs to take to school, so doesn't miss out on sports |
|  |  |  |  |
|  |  |  |  |
|  |  |  |  |

# What About Me?

Answer the following questions and write the answers in the thought bubbles.

What are some things I already do to get organized?

What are some things that I don't organize very well?

## WHAT DO OTHER PEOPLE THINK ABOUT ME?

Ask someone else the questions below and write their answers into the speech bubbles.

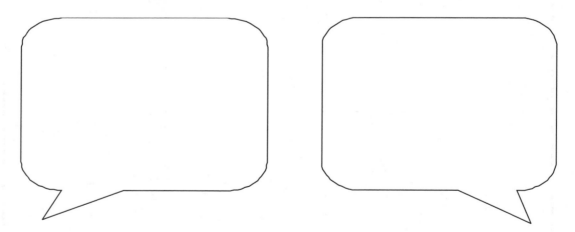

What are some things that you think I am already good at organizing?

What are some things that you think I don't organize very well?

# What If...?

If you could get better organized, what benefits would there be? Think about things like how much time you might have, how you might feel, how other people might feel, how much independence you could have, the number of arguments you might have or even how many things you could get finished! Fill this sheet in yourself, and then see what other people think, adding any good ideas they have. So, **if you could get better organized...**

What would be better at school?

What would be better at home?

During after-school activities?

Anywhere else? _____

# Bag Packing Challenge: Preparation

This challenge takes a bit of time to set up but it is worth it! It can be done in two ways:

1.  If you are already at high school or at a school that has a similar format (e.g. a timetable, you bring text books from home) then **use your own resources and timetable**.

2.  If you are not yet at high school or a similar school, **use the examples we have given you** unless you already have a copy of your subject lists and timetable. The examples you need are on the next page and will help you do the steps below.

**Step one**: Make a wall chart that lists ALL the things you need to take to school. The key things you need to include are:

*   things you should take EVERY day (e.g. diary, pencil case, wallet, lunch, keys)
*   things you need to take for each SUBJECT (e.g. text books, special equipment).

You might want to divide the list up using these headings (e.g. every day, Science, Maths).

**Step two**: Copy your weekly timetable onto another wall chart, making sure you can clearly see what things are on each day of the week. Add other regular commitments you have before, during or after school, such as after-school sports and lunch clubs.

**Step three**: Get out all the equipment, books and folders you would need throughout the week. If you are going to do this activity at school (where you don't have all your stuff), or you are using the example sheets on the next page, get creative and borrow items or put different labels on them (e.g. turn a 'Science' text book into 'Geography').

# Bag Packing Challenge: Examples If Needed

## WEEKLY TIMETABLE

| Monday | Tuesday | Wednesday | Thursday | Friday |
|---|---|---|---|---|
| Maths | Science | Sports (prac) | Science | Sports (prac) |
| Art | Maths | Sports (prac) | Science | English |
| **First break** | | | | |
| English | Maths | Art | English | Geography |
| Science | Music | Art | Music | Art |
| **Second break** | | | | |
| Sports (theory) | English | Geography | Maths | Science |
| Geography | English | Geography | Maths | Music |

## EQUIPMENT LIST FOR SUBJECTS

| | |
|---|---|
| English: | Text book, novel, exercise book |
| Science: | Text book, exercise book, folder |
| Maths: | Text book, exercise book, protractor, calculator |
| Sports (practice): | Sports clothes (e.g. shoes, socks, t-shirt, shorts) |
| Sports (theory): | Text book, exercise book |
| Geography: | Text book, exercise book, folder |
| Art: | Portfolio, folder |
| Music: | Folder, trumpet |

# Bag Packing Challenge: Action

Now you have done the preparation, you are ready for action – the time trials!

Start with an empty school bag and have all your equipment out. The adult you are with will call out a day of the week and start the timer. Using the wall charts you have made, pack into your bag everything you would need for that day as fast as you can. When the bag is zipped up, call out 'Done' and the timer is stopped. The other person then checks to see how you have gone. Start with 10 points and deduct 1 point for every item you forgot to pack and 1 point for every item you packed but didn't actually need to take! *Remember:* You are aiming for speed AND accuracy! Record your trials below and then highlight the one with the best results (fastest time and highest points):

| Trial | Day of the week | Time taken | Points (max 10) |
|-------|-----------------|------------|-----------------|
| 1     |                 |            |                 |
| 2     |                 |            |                 |
| 3     |                 |            |                 |

Is it easier if all your stuff for the one subject is kept together? _____

Do you think having the wall charts is easier than looking in your diary or trying to remember _____?

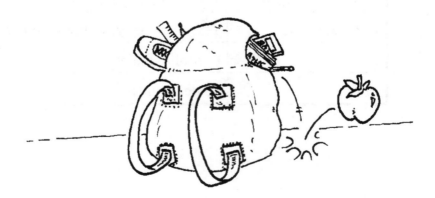

# Card Sorting Speed Trials

This activity will get you to start thinking about how organizing things in advance and having a system can make tasks easier and faster to complete. Cut the symbols from the next page into separate cards. The challenge is to sort them into piles so that each pile has the sequence drawn here. There are also some extra symbols to add a challenge! These need to be put aside and not accidentally included in the pattern! Do each trial and record the time taken.

TOP

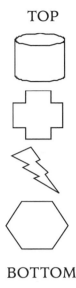

BOTTOM

### Trial 1: NO ORGANIZATION

- Shuffle the cards; spread them over the table face up.
- Start the timer and see how long it takes to sort them into piles of the sequence.

**Time taken:** _____

### Trial 2: PREPARATION AND GROUPING

- Before you start, sort the cards into piles of the same shape. Arrange them on the table so from left to right is: hexagon, cross, triangle, cylinder, diamond and lightning.
- Start the timer and see how long it takes to sort them into piles of the sequence.

**Time taken:** _____

### Trial 3: PREPARATION GROUPING AND ORDER

- Before you start, sort the cards into piles of the same shape and place them on the table in the same order as the pattern above; put the extra cards to one side as well.

**Time taken:** _____

**Discuss:** Which trial was fastest? Which trial was easiest? Why?

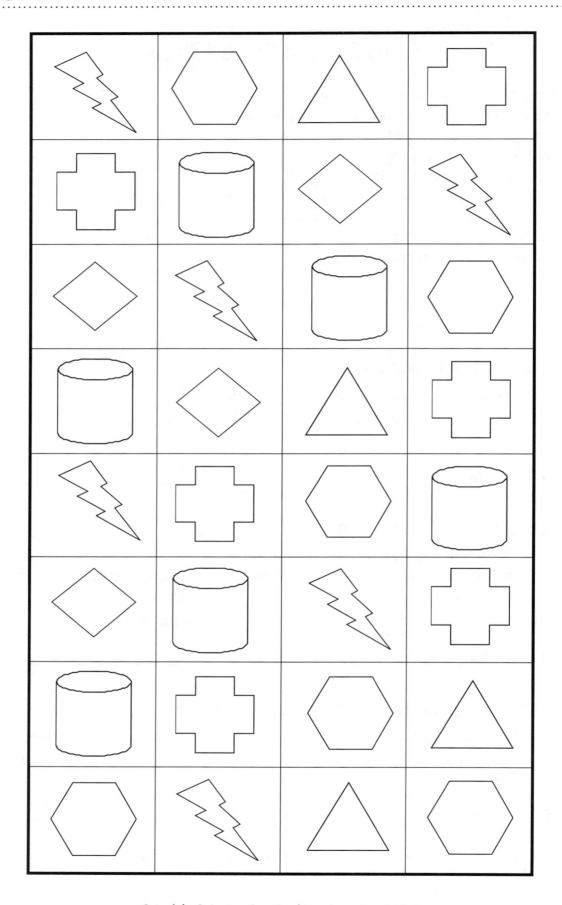

# What Could I Do If...?

Imagine yourself in the situations below and think about how you might respond. Before starting, read through the 'Top Tips for Young People' for some inside information!

**Situation 1:**
You have been asked to tidy your room and it is an absolute mess.

How can you break down this chore into smaller steps? Can you think of a good system to use?

_____

_____

How could you stay motivated to get it finished?

_____

Do you have any other ideas that might help?

_____


**Situation 2:**
You can never remember what homework you have and even though you can remember writing down your English homework and putting your Maths worksheet into your bag, you can never find them when you need them.

What can you do to better organize your homework? How could you store and transport it?

Instead of writing the answer, go to www.bubbl.us and make a 'mind map' on this topic. Start with 'organize homework' in the middle of the map and then put any ideas you have around this. Print it off and add it to your folder.

# Getting Sorted

Look back through the worksheets you have completed to help answer the questions below.

**Organization and me**

Times I am well organized: _____

Times I struggle to be organized: _____

Some of the good things about being organized: _____

**My top three strategies that help me get organized:**

1. _____

2. _____

3. _____

## WOULD ORGANIZATION BE A GOOD AREA TO WORK ON?

| Young person: | ☐ Yes | ☐ No | ☐ Maybe |
|---|---|---|---|
| Adult: | ☐ Yes | ☐ No | ☐ Maybe |

**If YES or MAYBE, see Chapter 9 for help with goal setting**

# 'What is Organization?' Answer Sheet

Does yours match the pattern below? If not, discuss the things you disagree on.

| | | | | |
|---|---|---|---|---|
| Having a system | Being boring | Never finding things | Forgetting things | Making time for fun |
| Knowing where stuff is | Having a place for things | Leaving things at home | Making things simple | Knowing what comes next |
| Using a schedule/diary | Not getting things finished | Having a plan | Being late | Thinking about the future |
| Having a routine | Getting to places on time | Just seeing what happens | Places to start and stop | Having the things you need |
| Making things stress free | Being a nerd | Starting wherever | Losing things | Breaking things into steps |

# Organization and Getting Sorted

A system takes time to set up, but it does make things easier and faster, giving you more time to have fun! You will probably need to test any system out, make some changes to it, and then give it time and practice to make it work really well for you. Here are some things you might want to try when you are getting sorted.

1. **Make things simple and visual:**

   - Only get out the things you need and put other stuff away.

   - Break things up into clear, achievable steps.

   - Make a wall chart or checklist so you can *see* what the steps are.

   - Use pictures instead of words to cut down on reading – use photos, symbols or images from clipart or the internet.

   - Colour code things, such as using green stickers on all maths books/homework.

   - Use diaries and calendars so you can *see* time frames (e.g. days, weeks), as well as deadlines and important events. Some people like special organizers or diaries as others like computer-based programs (e.g. Microsoft Outlook).

2. **Set up your space and equipment:**

   - Make sure things have a particular place to go.

   - Take a picture of how things should look and put it on the wall so you use this as a 'visual check'.

   - Have folders or plastic wallets to keep letters and worksheets in.

   - Use different sections of your bag (e.g. keys always in the same pocket).

   - Use a pencil case.

3.   **Have a system and get into a routine:**

- Do things in a set order and one step at a time, such as tidying your room like this:
    - dirty clothes in the basket
    - clean clothes away
    - shoes away
    - all games/CDs away
    - make the bed.
- Do things at a less stressful or busy time (e.g. pack your bag the night before).
- Create three trays for your homework: 'To Do', 'Working' and 'Finished'.

4.   **Set yourself time targets:**

- Make a set time to get certain things done (e.g. do chores at 6.30pm every night before your favourite TV show at 7.00pm).
- Set timers or alarms and try and get things done before they go off.
- Use music to help you judge time (e.g. get all the clothes put away before this song ends; tidy room for three songs).

5.   **Make things your own and have fun!**

- Design things so they are definitely yours: add pictures of yourself, downloaded images from the net or logos from your favourite teams/TV shows/computer games. Get creative with Word Art, clipart or other software programs.
- Have fun while you are doing things!

# Memory Tips

Being able to remember things doesn't just happen – we all need to use tricks to help our brain store information properly. Basically, the more you 'do' with information, the more chance you have of remembering it. For example, if you are trying to remember someone's name, rather than just saying the name to yourself you could find something to rhyme with it. You could also think about any friends or famous people who share that name. Some other tricks are the following:

- For things with lots of different steps: say them over and over again to yourself while listing off the steps on your fingers.

- Visualize yourself doing something – create a movie and *see* it happen with you as the star (e.g. going and buying the four things you need from the shop).

- Use mnemonics – memory tricks using very short poems or special words (e.g. 'I before E except after C', phrases to help remember the order of the planets).

- Ask yourself questions about information straight away to test your own memory (e.g. 'So what was the assignment again? When was it due?').

Other good memory strategies can be using reminders about what you need to do:

- Set an alarm on your mobile phone, your watch, or the oven timer.

- Put up a reminder sign where you will see it (e.g. sticky note on your door/bag).

- Write a checklist and then tick off the steps as you do them.

- Keep lists, and use diaries and calendars (paper or electronic).

Another great idea is to have a set routine so that you don't need to remember or think about the steps (e.g. so you can go on 'automatic pilot', like getting ready for bed).

- Do things the same way and in the same order each time (e.g. packing your bag).

- Put things in the same place; make a place for everything to belong.

# Getting Sorted: The Big Picture

Organization is a big topic and a significant issue in the lives of young people with ADHD and the people around them. There are lots of great strategies and the best tip of all is to give them a go! Get creative, spend the extra time at the start in setting up systems and then be prepared to 'tweak' them as you go. Remember that everyone organizes themselves differently and you need to find systems that work for the individual. These strategies often need some good marketing in order to engage the young person – you will have to sell the advantages (e.g. greater independence, less nagging, extra time)!

The key things to consider include the following:

- What is the priority? Keep each strategy focused on a specific target (e.g. homework routine, morning routine, managing homework/assignments, tidying bedroom).

- What bits can be pre-prepared (e.g. done the night before, using templates)?

- How can you set up the environment to make it easier (e.g. simple storage, colour coding)?

- How can you make reminders visual so you don't need to keep nagging (e.g. using photos, checklists, planners/calendars, contracts)?

- How can a task be broken down into different steps, each with a clear start and stop?

- How can the system be extended to include other people – the class or the family?

- Does the young person first need to be taught to use some of the solutions and tools we present to them (e.g. do they know how to use a diary effectively)?

- Computer-based tools such as Microsoft Outlook might be more motivating and also give clear visual representations (e.g. calendar and 'task list' system). Consider how the school and home can work together to enable access to these tools.

- How can we prompt the young person to continue the use of organization tools and strategies, and check they are being used effectively?

# Getting Sorted: Some Specifics

## AT HOME

The task of 'tidying the bedroom' can easily become an ongoing point of stress at home, and not just for those families who have a member with ADHD! It can be valuable to have an agreement about each person's space, and an open respect for the bedroom as a place to relax, create, escape and be yourself. Agreements can be made on how much mess can be tolerated, keeping in mind the reality of teenagers and remembering who has to actually live with the mess. Ultimately hygiene, health and safety are the biggest concerns. Pick your battles carefully!

## AT SCHOOL

Young people with ADHD find it difficult to organize their thoughts and analyse tasks or questions in a structured, logical and thorough way. There are many different ways to support this problem and some additional resources are identified at the end of this chapter. One tool that can be effective is 'mind mapping', which helps with organizing thoughts in a more visual way. To find out more on the use of mind maps look at:

- www.thinksmart.com (mind mapping in eight easy steps)
- http://wiki.classroom20.com (need to register but this is free and has lesson plans on how to use and teach mind mapping)
- www.jcu.edu.au/office/tld/learningskills/mindmap/index.html (good introduction and examples of how to use)
- www.buzanworld.com (about the creator)
- www.bubbl.us (an easy-to-use website that will help you create mind maps).

# Getting Sorted

## BOOKS

- *Learning to Slow Down and Pay Attention: A Book for Kids about ADHD* by Kathleen Nadeau and Ellen Dixon, 2004, American Psychological Association.

- *The 'Putting on the Brakes' Activity Book for Young People with ADHD* by Patricia Quinn and Judith Stern, 1993, Magination Press.

## INTERNET SITES

- Suite 101, addadhd.suite101.com (no www before!); log on to site and search for 'Classroom strategies'; choose 'Classroom Strategies for ADHD'.

- ADDitude; Living Well with ADD and Learning Disabilities: www.additudemag.com/adhd/article/980.html (additional articles at this site).

## TECHNOLOGY AND TOOLS

- Timers that give clear visual feedback on the passing of time (www.timetimer.com)

- Software programs that help to structure learning such as Inspiration (www.inspiration.com), which helps to plan, organize, research and present.

- Calendars and planning tools: these can be computer based (e.g. Microsoft Outlook, www.yourorganiser.com.au), utilize portable technology (e.g. linked to mobile phones/PDA) or paper diaries/organizers with additional structure (e.g. Tudor Organizer, Planner Pad).

## EXECUTIVE DYSFUNCTION AND ADHD

- Teens with ADHD: www.chrisdendy.com/executive.htm

- About Kids Health: www.aboutkidshealth.ca (search ADHD Executive Dysfunction)

- A New Understanding of Attention Deficit Disorder: www.drthomasebrown.com/brown_model/index.html

# Friends and Mates

It would be easy to think that the concept of friendship does not need much introduction. Yet each one of us is likely to have a very different understanding of this term, and have experienced a diverse range of friendships throughout our lives. Young people are exposed to many images of friendship through TV shows, the relationships modelled by parents and siblings, as well as through other young people at school and in their neighbourhood. In supporting young people to reflect on this important topic, it may be beneficial to take stock of some of the key concepts that underpin friendships. These are often discussed openly when children first start school, but there are very few 're-freshers' as they grow!

In essence, a friendship is a relationship between two people that is based on mutual pleasure and is caring in nature. Some key concepts that you may want to clarify include the following:

- Friendships should be a two-way process with give and take on both sides.

- Your friends will change over time as your interests and lifestyle change.

- What makes a friendship will change over time, as relationships and social networks develop and become more complex.

- At any one time you will have different types of friendships with different people (e.g. do different things together, spend more or less time together).

- It is important to have a network of support through friendships across school, home and the community.

- Some young people aren't worried about having friends and prefer to do most things by themselves; this is OK if the person is happy.

- Friendships take work and will not always be easy; sometimes friends disagree and this is OK if they both work to resolve these issues.

As we know through our own life experiences, making and keeping friends is a complex skill that relies on a lot of underlying factors, including social skills, communication skills and self-esteem.

## ADHD AND FRIENDSHIPS

ADHD may impact on a young person's ability to make and keep friends in a number of ways. Some of the friendship problems described by parents and teachers are associated with the key features of ADHD – impulsivity, poor attention and restlessness. These young people can appear unpredictable, making others wary of them or even scared/worried in their company. Their impulsive actions, such as snatching things, talking over the top of you and starting something before you have finished talking, can seem rude. Similarly, it can be frustrating to hang out and play with someone who keeps changing the game before it has finished, or who can't remember things you have already talked about and agreed on! Young people with ADHD can also seem bossy as they often try to control games and have difficulty listening. Who can deny that it can be annoying to be with someone who is always noisy, fidgeting, over-excited and just can't seem to sit down and relax?

Although listing these problems can seem quite negative, it is important to think about these issues, as they are part of the reality of life with ADHD and are often over-looked. The other matters to consider are not in themselves inherent to ADHD, but are common 'knock on' effects of living with this condition. These young people tend to get into trouble regularly at school (for talking, not paying attention, not completing work…) and can be seen by others as 'naughty kids' and therefore avoided by some of their peers.

This same factor can also make them seem like desirable company for other young people who may also struggle to follow the rules at school (i.e. the 'bad influences'!). Indeed, young people with ADHD are often easily led by others. They also typically try to mask the fact that they are struggling by using strategies such as acting 'the clown' (mainly boys) or withdrawing and staying quiet (mainly girls). These coping mechanisms can in fact make it harder for them to make and maintain good friendships. In their attempt to fit in, be accepted and have friends, young people with ADHD are often highly socially vulnerable.

## CHALLENGES AT HIGH SCHOOL

As with all the other topics we have discussed in this book, the move to high school is associated with increased demands on the social skills needed by the young person in this domain, and reduced external support from adults. Throughout the teenage years, friendships become more complex and distinct social groups are formed. Lunch time becomes more about socializing and interacting than doing or playing together. Relationships between the sexes also change, adding a range of new challenges. For most children, friendships become a means through which they develop their identity, gain support (real and emotional) and feel part of a community. It could be argued that positive friendships play as powerful a role in promoting happiness and success as any of the other support strategies outlined in this book.

## OBJECTIVES

The focus of this chapter is on two specific areas that can create initial challenges in the high school setting. First, in the skills required to meet and befriend new classmates, and second, in learning to deal with teasing and bullying. These are only very small skill sets within this very large field, and we highly recommend that you explore the resources at the end of this chapter for additional support ideas. In particular, conflict resolution, negotiation and assertiveness skills are often ideal areas for further intervention.

The worksheets and advice sheets in this chapter are designed to support the following processes:

1. To help the young person think about what friendship is, the qualities involved in being a good friend and traits within their own friendships.

2. To create an opportunity to practise basic social and communication skills which are useful, particularly when meeting new people.

3. To help the young person to reflect on this matter of teasing and bullying.

4. To encourage your child to consider how to deal with teasing and bullying in a positive and safe way.

# You and Your Friends

Friendships are an important part of school life, particularly if you are starting at a new school. Let's think together about your friendships at the moment by circling your answers to the quick quiz below.

| | | | |
|---|---|---|---|
| 1. Are you happy with your current friendships? | Yes | Sometimes | No |
| 2. Do you have a close friend? | Yes | Sometimes | No |
| 3. Would you like to have more friends? | Yes | Sometimes | No |
| 4. Do you have friends at school? | Yes | Sometimes | No |
| 5. Do you have friends in your neighbourhood? | Yes | Sometimes | No |
| 6. Do you have friends at after-school clubs/sports? | Yes | Sometimes | No |
| 7. Do you go to your friends' homes; do they come to yours? | Yes | Sometimes | No |
| 8. Do you find it easy to make friends? | Yes | Sometimes | No |
| 9. Do you find it easy to keep friends? | Yes | Sometimes | No |
| 10. Do you argue with your friends? | Yes | Sometimes | No |

Which of the following 'friendship traits' do you show? Tick your answer. Remember to be honest!

- ☐ Good listener
- ☐ Good advice giver
- ☐ Honest
- ☐ Good at solving problems
- ☐ Say kind things to people
- ☐ Generous
- ☐
- ☐

- ☐ Caring
- ☐ Trustworthy
- ☐ Understanding
- ☐ Fun
- ☐ Don't hold grudges
- ☐ Thoughtful
- ☐
- ☐

Are there any other 'friendship traits' that you think you have? Add them to the list!

# Ups and Downs of Friendships

Think of one of your good friends and fill in the section below:

My good friend _____ (name)

What do you enjoy doing together?

_____

_____

What makes them your good friend? What do you do for them? What do they do for you?

_____

_____

_____

⇧ ⇩ ⇧ ⇩ ⇧ ⇩ ⇧ ⇩

Think of a time when you had a problem with a friend and fill in the section below: What problem did you have with this friend? How did you work it out?

_____

_____

You may have noticed other people have problems with friends; it's a pretty common thing. Can you think of someone you know who had a problem with a friend? What did they do?

_____

_____

It is normal to have some friendships that only last for a little while, and some that just don't work out. What do you think about this? Discuss your thoughts and experiences.

# Exploring Teasing and Bullying

Now that you have thought about friendships, it might be useful to consider something that is not a friendly thing to do – bullying or teasing. Complete this worksheet to help you become better at detecting bullies.

Teasing or bullying can happen in many different ways. Carly has put down some of her ideas on how people can be bullied or teased, and now it is your turn to add your own ideas.

- Being called names.
- Being ignored or left out.
- Getting nasty or threatening emails, text messages or chat messages.
- 
- 
- 

## QUICK QUIZ

Circle your answers to the following questions so that you can think about some of your own experiences. Remember to be honest!

| | | | |
|---|---|---|---|
| Have you ever been bullied? | Yes | No | Maybe |
| Have you ever seen someone else getting bullied? | Yes | No | Maybe |
| Do you think bullying is a problem? | Yes | No | Maybe |
| Have you ever picked on or teased someone else? | Yes | No | Maybe |
| Have you ever joined in with others who were bullying? | Yes | No | Maybe |
| Have you ever reported bullying to a teacher? | Yes | No | Maybe |
| Do you think we should just go along with bullying? | Yes | No | Maybe |

# Cartoon Strip

Can you think of a time when you may have been teased, picked on or bullied? Or maybe a time when you yourself have done this to someone else? Think about what you were thinking and feeling. How do you think the other person felt? Draw out what happened in the cartoon strip on the next page. You only have four 'frames' so plan what will be in each one. The first frame needs to be how the teasing started and the last frame needs to be what happened afterwards. You could use the characters provided on this page by choosing a body and adding in their faces, hair, clothes, etc. You can photocopy them (and cut and paste), trace them or just try to draw them yourself. Don't forget to use speech bubbles to show what people are saying and thought bubbles to show what people are thinking.

**Have fun!**

What have you learnt from doing this? Maybe you have some thoughts about what it feels like to be bullied? Or what it feels like to BE the bully? Why might people bully others? Discuss this and write down any important ideas you have:

# Friendship Wordsearch

Fourteen friendship words are hidden in the grid below. Why don't you practise one of your attention and concentration strategies from the 'Don't Miss A Thing!' chapter and see if you can complete the wordsearch in five minutes! Check your answers using the answer sheet in the 'Top Tips for Young People' at the end of the chapter.

| T | Y | A | L | P | F | J | E | K | L |
|---|---|---|---|---|---|---|---|---|---|
| R | A | G | O | A | R | M | L | A | C |
| U | S | E | H | R | I | Y | A | R | S |
| S | H | F | R | T | E | O | M | T | K |
| T | A | N | U | Y | N | W | Y | F | E |
| F | R | I | E | N | D | L | P | R | O |
| N | E | M | X | B | S | M | I | L | E |
| G | R | G | L | P | H | A | I | W | V |
| T | C | U | S | J | I | T | A | L | K |
| A | K | H | E | L | P | F | U | L | C |
| C | M | C | A | R | I | N | G | I | E |

Words to search for:

| | |
|---|---|
| CALM | MATE |
| CARING | PARTY |
| FRIEND | PLAY |
| FRIENDSHIP | SHARE |
| FUN | SMILE |
| HELPFUL | TALK |
| HUG | TRUST |

# Communication is the Key: Listening

You may have noticed that being able to communicate and share things is a really important friendship skill. Now you get to practise two really easy but important communication tricks.

## LISTENING

If you listen to people well, it shows that you are interested and it makes them feel good to be around you. Now you have a chance to get some practice! Ask someone to talk for three minutes about something that they are really interested in. It could be anything! Put on a timer or a stopwatch to time the three minutes. You have to do all of the following things while the other person talks. Tick them off as you go.

| | | |
|---|---|---|
| Look at their eyes but don't stare – slowly move from eye to nose ☐ | Check anything you missed or didn't understand – 'Where is that?' ☐ | Nod your head ☐ |
| Turn your body towards them, lean forward a bit ☐ | Make agreeing noises, say 'wow/yeah/crazy!' ☐ | Smile ☐ |

How many did you do? Ask the speaker how it felt to have a good listener.

Now it is your turn to talk for three minutes on *your* favourite thing. The other person needs to do the OPPOSITE of all the good listening signs (e.g. turn body away, don't say anything, frown).

How did it go? How does it feel when someone doesn't show they are listening?

# Communication is the Key: 'I' Statements

## 'I' STATEMENTS': SAYING WHAT YOU FEEL

It is also really important to be able to say what you feel without hurting other people's feelings or getting angry. One really good way of doing this is by using a handy trick called an 'I' Statement. These have a special formula that goes like this:

1. **State the problem**: 'When I didn't hear about your birthday party...'

2. **State how you feel**: '...I felt really hurt...'

3. **State what you want the person to do differently next time**: '...and next time I would like you to talk to me first.'

The trick is to talk about things from *your* perspective (the 'I') so that other people can understand your side of things and not feel like you are blaming them.

**Practise saying 'I' statements to another person for these scenarios:**

1. You are left out of the football game at lunch time.

2. Your friends don't pick you to be in their group for a History project.

3. You hear one of your friends say that they think your brother/sister is a loser.

Ask the other person how they felt when you made your 'I' statements. How did you feel saying them? Did you feel in control, cool, calm and collected?

# Making New Friends

At high school you meet lots of new people, especially in the first few weeks or when you start a new class. This worksheet helps you think about things to say and questions to ask people when you want to get to know them better or become friends. Find someone to practise your questions on so that you will then be ready for any chance that might come. Make sure you also remember to use your listening skills!

## Introducing yourself

- Hi. My name is _____

- I am really into _____

- My favourite sports team is _____

Think of two other things you could say:

- _____

- _____

## What would you like to ask them?

- What is your name? _____

- What is your favourite TV show? _____

- What sort of music are you into? _____

Think of two other questions you could ask:

- _____

- _____

**Tips to remember**: Introduce yourself, ask the other person questions and share information about yourself. Then check to see if it is going well. Is the other person listening to you (remember the signs of listening)? If yes, you might want to ask them to meet up another time to do something. If not, that's OK – find someone else to meet!

# Keeping Things Friendly

Sometimes having friends can be hard. Friends may do things which upset you, like not inviting you to things or making jokes about you. Write down or draw about a time that a friend hurt your feelings.

Now write down some things that you could have done to make the situation better. Remember to think about any strategies you have learnt that help with coping with stress or communicating with friends, and look through some books or tip sheets to get some new ideas – the more the better!

# Responding to Teasing and Bullying

Imagine that you work for *What's Up* Magazine as the Agony Aunt or Uncle. You receive the letter below. Write out a reply advising Carly on what she should do.

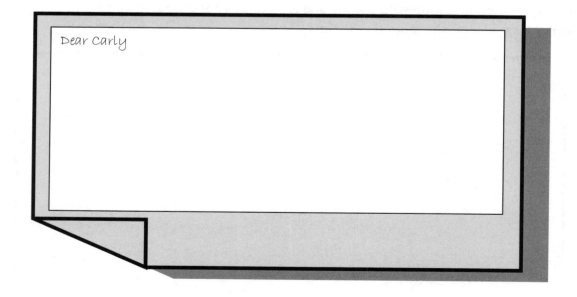

Dear What's Up Magazine

I hope you can help me. I am 11 years old and have recently started at a new school. When I started at the school I made friends with 3 girls, but it turns out they are not really friends at all. They have started sending me text messages on my phone saying that I'm a loser and if I want to be their friend I should bring them money. I'm really unhappy and don't know what to do or who to talk to. Please help.

Carly

Dear Carly

# What Could I Do If...?

Imagine yourself in the situations below and think about how you might respond using the ideas you have learnt from this chapter of the book.

**Situation 1:**
It is your first day at your new school. You arrive at your classroom before the teacher gets there and so you sit down at a spare desk. There is a person next to you who is also early, but you have never met them before. What could you say to them?

_____

_____

_____

**Situation 2:**
You are walking home from school when a guy from your Maths class and some of his mates come up to you and start giving you a hard time about your new haircut and calling you names. Then they start walking off laughing. What could you do?

_____

_____

_____

# Friends and Mates

Look back through the worksheets you have completed to help answer the questions below.

**My top three strategies to make and keep friends:**

1. _____

2. _____

3. _____

**My top two strategies to stop teasing and bullying:**

1. _____

2. _____

## WOULD MAKING FRIENDS BE A GOOD AREA TO WORK ON?

| Young person: | ☐ Yes | ☐ No | ☐ Maybe |
|---|---|---|---|
| Adult: | ☐ Yes | ☐ No | ☐ Maybe |

**If YES or MAYBE, see Chapter 9 for help with goal setting**

# 'Friendship Wordsearch' Answer Sheet

**How did you go? Did you find them all?**

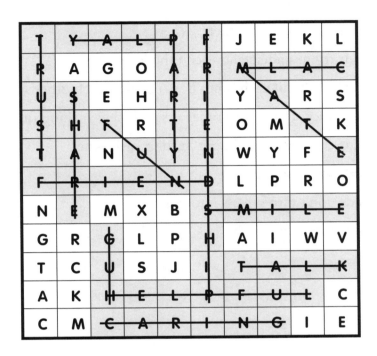

# Top Ten Qualities of a Good Friend

1.  Good friends care about each other.

2.  Good friends help each other sort out problems.

3.  Good friends listen to each other.

4.  Good friends try to understand each other's feelings.

5.  Good friends don't put each other down or hurt each other's feelings.

6.  Good friends stick up for each other if someone is making fun of them.

7.  Good friends can disagree without hurting each other.

8.  Good friends are trustworthy.

9.  Good friends don't turn secrets into gossip.

10.  Good friends have fun together!

# Bullying

**What to do if you are being bullied:**

- No-one deserves to be bullied, so don't feel embarrassed or ashamed.

- It is important to talk to someone you trust and feel comfortable with about what is going on. This could be a friend, parent, carer, teacher or youth worker.

- Tell the person what has been happening and how it is making you feel. Hopefully you will be able to think together about what to do next. If talking to this person doesn't seem to help, you may have to speak to someone else. Just don't give up!

- If you are being bullied at school you could check out the school's guidelines and rules on bullying. You may be able to access these on your school's website or otherwise you could ask a teacher for a copy.

**What to do if you think someone else is being bullied:**

- Remember no-one deserves to be bullied, so don't ignore what is happening.

- Try and talk to the person you think is being bullied and let them know you are worried about the situation and that it needs to be dealt with. Encourage them to talk to someone who can help, such as a parent, teacher or a youth worker.

- If the person who is being bullied doesn't want to talk to anyone, you may need to report what you saw anyway. It may be possible for you to do this anonymously by writing a note about what you saw.

**Want to know more?**

- Check out the websites in the 'Resources section' of this chapter for more tips on dealing with bullying.

# Friends and Mates

We all want young people to have good friends and be good friends to others, but often forget that they have to learn the skills involved. If a young person with ADHD is having particular difficulty in getting along with their peers and establishing a social network, you might try the following:

- **Identifying a buddy or mentor** from an older year group at school. The buddy can keep an eye on the young person during break times, and perhaps spend one break a week with them in order to role-model positive social behaviour.

- **Participation in lunch-time activity clubs** for structured and supported social interactions.

- **Implementing specific stress management systems** that allow timely withdrawal in order to avoid public 'meltdowns' (e.g. a 'time out' pass that allows them to leave the classroom or lunch hall in a quick and calm way if they are feeling stressed; see the 'Keeping Cool and Calm!' chapter for more ideas).

- **Teaching and modelling** some of the more complex social skills as 'real-life' situations and challenges emerge (e.g. conflict resolution, tolerance).

- **Creating opportunities for one-to-one social interaction** with others as this is an easier setting in which to practise, learn and problem solve. For example, working in pairs at school rather than small groups, and encouraging friends to visit individually at home.

- **Involvement in sporting and recreational groups.** Typically individual sports (e.g. swimming, martial arts) are less stressful than team-based sports and still create good social opportunities. Non-competitive groups such as Scouts are also ideal.

- **Setting a good example!** Young people are always watching how the adults around them relate to others, so make sure you are setting a good example. Talk through your own experiences so that they can see that these things aren't always easy, and that there is thought, choice and effort behind our actions.

# Friends and Mates

## BOOKS

- *The Straight Talk Manual: A Self-Esteem and Life Skills Workbook for Young People (5th Edition)* by Diane Brokenshire, 2001, Straight Talk Publishing.

- *Talkabout Relationships – Building Self-Esteem and Relationship Skills* by Alex Kelly, 2004, Speechmark Publishing Ltd.

- *How to Handle Bullies, Teasers, and Other Meanies: A Book That Takes the Nuisance Out of Name Calling and Other Nonsense* by Kate Cohen-Posey, 1995, Rainbow Books.

## INTERNET SITES

- Bullying UK: www.bullying.co.uk
- ChildLine: www.childline.org.uk
- Bullying. No Way!: www.bullyingnoway.com.au

# CHAPTER 8

# Surviving Homework!

Homework is one of those issues that can easily become a challenge for any young person. As a result, it can also develop into a point of conflict between them and the individuals supporting them at home and school.

## ADHD AND HOMEWORK

Just as ADHD impacts on the ability to focus on, organize and complete work at school, it influences a young person's ability to complete homework tasks. However, there are a number of additional factors that make homework even more challenging, including:

- Reduced supervision provided by adults for this task, resulting in greater demands for monitoring their own attention/focus.

- Limited available help in structuring and organizing themselves, including problem solving individual homework tasks and also coordinating and prioritizing their overall homework and assignment load.

- Impact of fatigue after a long day at school – remember that these young people need to work extra hard all day just to focus for short periods of time.

- Internal drive to seek movement and stimulation, which is even stronger after a day of sitting down at school.

- Desire to have fun and attempt easy tasks with guaranteed success, particularly after a day of struggling at school with limited choice/control.

Together, these considerations pose significant hurdles. It may take additional planning and support to ensure that the young person with ADHD can either clear these or negotiate around them!

## CHALLENGES AT HIGH SCHOOL

It is widely recognized that the volume of homework dramatically increases at high school. In addition, young people are expected to organize multiple projects and juggle various deadlines with few reminders. Often these increased demands are also competing with a more complex life outside school, including sports, hobbies, friendships and steps towards greater independence. Some of the common difficulties seen include:

- problems recording homework – not written down, written down incorrectly, or unable to locate where it is written down

- avoidance, procrastination and/or opposition to completing homework at home

- rushed homework completion with poor quality of work

- difficulties organizing work – not knowing when things are due, not recognizing how long things will take, forgetting projects and deadlines
- forgetting to take homework to school or to hand it in.

## OBJECTIVES

The worksheets and advice sheets in this chapter are designed to support the following processes:

1. To help the young person reflect on their feelings about homework and their current homework habits.

2. To enable the young person to learn about a range of support strategies for homework and to try these out.

3. To integrate strategies from other sections of the book to help facilitate homework completion (particularly from the 'Don't Miss A Thing!' and 'Getting Sorted' chapters).

4. To problem solve around possible techniques for use in daily life.

# Homework Fears

It is pretty normal to have some worries or fears about the homework you might have to do when you start a new school, a new class or move up a year. James has started the list below, and now it is your turn to add your worries about homework underneath:

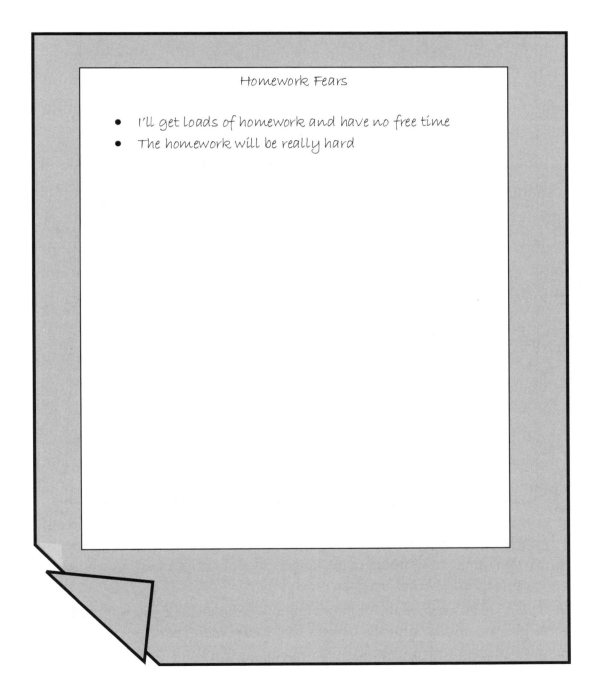

Homework Fears

- I'll get loads of homework and have no free time
- The homework will be really hard

# Why Homework?

It is important to think about what the point of homework is, and why it needs to be done. Write your ideas on the jigsaw below to help you think about the reasons why homework exists.

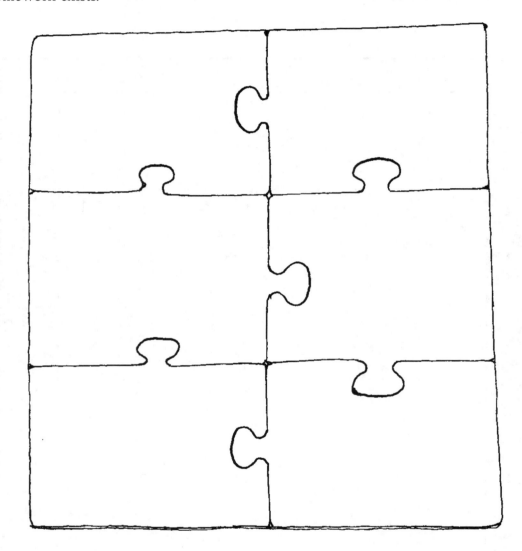

Read through the following questions and discuss your answers:

- Do you think that learning to get homework done might teach you other important skills? What are some examples?

- Think about whether any of these skills might be useful if you want to learn to play a musical instrument or train hard in a specific sport.

- Are there similarities with the skills that might also be needed when you get a job or do study once you have finished school?

# Quick Homework Quiz

1. What do you think about homework? Circle one answer:

(a) I hate all homework (b) I don't mind some homework (c) I like all homework

2. What is your best subject for homework and why?

_____

3. What is your worst subject for homework and why?

_____

4. Do you have any of these homework problems? Circle the right answer:

| | | | |
|---|---|---|---|
| I forget what homework needs to be done | Never | Sometimes | A lot |
| I forget to take my homework to school | Never | Sometimes | A lot |
| I argue with my parents/carers about homework | Never | Sometimes | A lot |
| I don't have my homework done on time | Never | Sometimes | A lot |
| I get into trouble at school about homework | Never | Sometimes | A lot |

5. Do you get help for your homework at school?     YES or NO?

   If Yes, what sort of help? _____

6. Do you get help for your homework at home?     YES or NO?

   If Yes, what sort of help? _____

# Homework: The Good Times

There are going to be good times when it comes to homework, even if you don't like it much or find it hard to get motivated. An example of a good time might have been when you finished it quickly, maybe didn't find it so difficult or earned good feedback from your teacher. Think of a time when you **recently** managed to complete a piece of homework and were happy with how you did. Use this example to help you fill in this worksheet.

- What was the homework task?

  _____

  _____

- Where did you do this piece of homework (including what room)?

  _____

  _____

- What time of day was it when you worked on your homework?

  _____

  _____

- What did you do just before you sat down to do it?

  _____

  _____

- Can you think of any extra things that might have helped you to do this homework well (e.g. worked with someone else, used the computer, was really interested in the topic, could get an award or reward, was being marked on the homework)?

  _____

  _____

# Concentration and Homework

Take a look back at the worksheets you completed in the 'Don't Miss A Thing!' chapter (particularly the 'Pulling It Together' sheets). Could any of the concentration strategies be useful when you are trying to complete your homework? Add any others that you can think of!

**Concentration strategies to help me with my homework:**

1.

2.

3.

# The Battle of Chaos v Calm

This is a fun way of working out how important it is to get your homework set up just right. Choose an activity that you need to concentrate on and that will take about five minutes. It could be a worksheet, a puzzle or copying down a page from a book. You need to find two versions of this activity, and then practise one in CHAOS and the other in CALM as outlined below.

| BATTLE 1 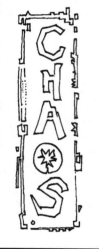 | Set up this space to work in: <br>• radio on loud <br>• sit with window in front of you <br>• sit on chair that's too high – with your feet dangling <br>• desk covered in stuff <br>• someone reading out aloud/talking <br>• someone walking close by | **Reflections:** <br>What did it feel like? <br><br>How well did you do the task? <br><br>What did the other person see you doing? |
| --- | --- | --- |
| BATTLE 2  | Set up this space to work in: <br>• quiet area <br>• desk facing blank wall <br>• clear desk top <br>• chair/desk correct height <br>• no-one walking/talking nearby | **Reflections:** <br>What did it feel like? <br><br>How well did you do the task? <br><br>What did the other person see you doing? |

# Where and When?

As you saw in 'The Battle of Chaos v Calm', your surroundings can really affect your ability to concentrate. Designing an environment and routine specifically to fit *you* can make a huge difference to your homework, and the next two worksheets will help you do just that!

## STEP 1: WHERE?

Before starting make sure you read the Top Tips on 'Setting Up a Homework Station'. Then think about the perfect 'set up' for you – it needs to be just right to help *you* to focus and get work done. Draw the details into the picture below, adding labels and comments. Think about: furniture, what is in front of you, where windows/doors are, what else is in the room, who is around, noise, equipment (computers, etc.) and where you would store things!

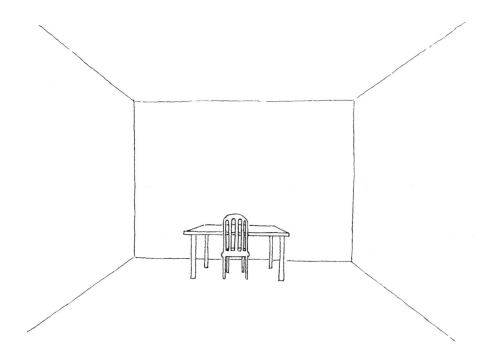

Have a look at this picture and compare it to where you are currently doing your homework. Are there many differences? If yes, is there a space that you could possibly arrange so it is like the picture? It could be at home, school or in the library.

Now you have thought about where to do homework, it is time to think about when!

## STEP 2: WHEN?

Try to think about your best time of day to get homework done. One of the most common times for homework is some time between finishing school and having the evening meal. Make up a 'typical' schedule for your life after school and write it on a scrap piece of paper. Make sure you include after-school clubs/care, snacks and dinner, TV/computer time, and sports. The aim is to find at **least an hour** where you can add in definite homework time. Write the final version into the planner below. One great trick is to make sure you do something that you like straight after your homework (e.g. ride your bike, play on the PlayStation, watch a TV show).

| Time | Planner: 'Typical' activities PLUS homework time |
|------|--------------------------------------------------|
| | Finish school and go _____ |
| | |
| | |
| | |
| | |
| | |
| | |
| | Get ready and go to bed |

Are there any other times of day when you could do your homework? Do you think these would work for you? What happens on the weekend?

# Homework Deals

We all have to do things that we don't really like or want to do. It might be the washing up, having to visit boring relatives, going next door to ask for your ball back or doing homework. Often the thing that gets us through these tasks **is thinking about a reward or good thing that could be enjoyed at the end**. These thoughts go like this… So maybe after I've washed up I'll be able to watch my favourite TV show and Mum will be really happy with me. If I visit my Auntie, I will get to eat some of the cake she always has; and, if I go next door for my ball, I can keep practising so I play really well this Saturday.

So what reward or good thing could come out of doing your homework…?

Use the table below to interview three people you know to discover how they reward themselves after doing a boring or horrible activity.

| Name | Boring/horrible task | Reward |
|---|---|---|
|  |  |  |
|  |  |  |
|  |  |  |

Now think about how you can reward yourself after finishing your homework. Remember – it needs to be something you can treat yourself to every day (so it can't be expensive!). Maybe you can strike a deal with your parents or carers?

# Homework: It's a Juggling Act

Sometimes you might be given two or three pieces of homework on the same day for different subjects. It is important to learn how to juggle these and figure out what to do first! The activity below will help you practise prioritizing your homework.

James can do one hour of homework each weeknight, except on Tuesdays when he can only do half an hour because of football practice. Below is an extract from James' homework diary and a blank homework planner. Can you plan out James' time so that he gets everything done on time?

| Day given | Homework |
|---|---|
| Monday | 1 hr Maths – due Wednesday + ½ hr History due Thursday |
| Tuesday | 1 hr French due Thursday |
| Wednesday | ½ hr Art + ½ hr English both due Friday |
| Thursday | 1 hr Science due next Monday |
| Friday | No homework! ☺ |

|  | Monday | Tuesday | Wednesday | Thursday | Friday |
|---|---|---|---|---|---|
| Subject |  |  |  |  |  |
| Time allowed |  |  |  |  |  |

# Homework MC

Sometimes people find it useful to have a short rap or rhyme they can say to themselves when they are finding something tough. This can help you feel better and have a laugh about a difficult task. It is a bit like the 'positive self-talk' you practised in the 'Feeling Great!' chapter. We have come up with two short raps that acknowledge that, while homework is annoying, it's better to get it over with and to focus on the benefits. Can you come up with your own rap that you can use to help you get through your homework? You can even choose a favourite song or rhythm to hum it along to!

'Homework is a pain, but there's a long-term gain.
I'll do well in school and it will all be cool.'

'Homework stinks but we've **all** got to do it,
Cause I'm tough, I know I can get through it.
Don't want to stress, just need to do it!'

_____

_____

_____

_____

# What Could I Do If…?

Imagine yourself in the situations below, and think about how you might respond using the ideas you have learnt from this chapter of the book.

**Situation 1:**

Every evening you seem to get into a massive fight with your parents over homework. They keep nagging you, telling you to 'start your homework' and asking how much you have and when it is due. This makes everyone stressed out for the whole evening. What could you do to get your parents off your back?

_____

_____

_____

**Situation 2:**

Some days you need to use the computer for your homework, but the computer is downstairs at the other end of the room where the TV is. Your brothers and sisters are always there watching DVDs and it drives you crazy when you are trying to get something done. Most days you give up and find something else to do. How could you try to solve this?

_____

_____

_____

# Surviving Homework!

Look back through the worksheets you have completed to help answer the questions below.

**What are some of the important things about:**

The times when you do your homework well?

_____

The times you struggle with your homework?

_____


**My top three strategies to help with my homework:**


1.  _____

2.  _____

3.  _____


### WOULD HOMEWORK BE A GOOD AREA
### TO WORK ON?

| Young person: | ☐ Yes | ☐ No | ☐ Maybe |
|---|---|---|---|
| Adult: | ☐ Yes | ☐ No | ☐ Maybe |

**If YES or MAYBE, see Chapter 9 for help with goal setting**

# Making a Homework Plan

Other young people have found it useful to develop a homework plan that helps pull together the ideas from this chapter of the book. You might also want to speak to your friends or older brothers/sisters and see what sorts of things they do to help get their homework done.

When it comes to writing your plan, some important things to include could be:

- where you will write down the homework you have been given in class
- how much time you will spend on your homework (for each night and the weekend)
- where you will complete your homework
- what time of day you will complete your homework
- how you will structure your homework time to help you concentrate (e.g. have regular breaks, start with the hardest work first, use a checklist)
- how you will organize your homework so that you remember to take the right books home with you and take the right piece of work to school on the right day
- how your parents might be able to help with parts of your homework, such as helping you plan and map out essays, or helping to organize your calendar and due dates
- when your parent or carer can check your homework diary or homework to make sure you are keeping up without having to nag you about this all the time
- making a list of classmates to call if you forget details or have questions
- what rewards you will give yourself after you have completed a piece of homework.

When you write your plan it is a good idea to get everyone to agree to it (and maybe even sign it) and then put it somewhere where everyone can check it as a reminder.

# Setting Up a Homework Station

The tips below might help you to design your own homework space.

**Furniture and equipment:**

- Make sure that the chair and table you use are the right height for you, so your feet can go flat on the ground (stops dangling and is more comfortable) and the table is around elbow height when sitting down. Try height-adjustable chairs such as office chairs, or make footstools out of telephone directories.

- Try using a computer to complete your homework. Remember that the school needs to agree to this first.

- Create space to do some work standing up. This could be standing at the table, working on a high shelf or at a whiteboard/wall chart.

- Have drawers, suspension files or boxes to store things in so your desk is clear.

**Blocking out visual distractions:**

- If you are sharing a large table with your brothers or sisters, try screening off a section each (e.g. use large ring binders opened up and Blu-Tacked to the table).

- Try putting the table or desk against a wall so you are facing a blank space.

- Use furniture to screen off your homework area (e.g. book case or screen to one side).

- Try using desk lamps if you don't like fluorescent lights or can see them flickering (e.g. use LED bulbs instead).

**Blocking out sound distractions:**

- Wear headphones with quiet music playing or without any music at all (just to block out sounds). Disposable ear-plugs can also be good.

- Find a space away from the TV, radio, road, etc.

- Have set 'quiet times' at home. Can other people wear headphones when watching TV/playing on the computer, to help this?

### Blocking out other distractions:

- Have a 'no mobile phone' policy during homework hours.
- If you are on the computer make sure that messaging and email services are turned off.
- Agree a family rule that you are only interrupted for emergencies or to help with or check homework.
- Keep a note pad to write down any thoughts you have on other topics – this helps to clear your mind but makes sure you won't forget the ideas.

### Get the details right:

- Use desk organizers for pens/pencils/erasers. Have a second set of these basics so that you can have a school pencil case that stays in your bag (buy a cool pencil case that you like and will use because they are really handy!).
- Have a space to put up a 'to do' checklist (for that day) and a homework planner/calendar (for the week). You may want to use a corkboard or whiteboard.
- Keep a small number of fidgets at your desk and a sports top water bottle.
- Keep on top of time – have a clock close by and consider timers to keep you on track.

# Surviving Homework!

If homework is a challenge for a young person with ADHD, consider the following tips:

- The school, parents/carers and the young person can meet to share ideas and develop a **joint homework plan** with support across both the home and school settings.

- Work towards the young person becoming more **independent** and taking on responsibility for their work. Tools like timetables and checklists can help with this.

- Identify a **'mentor' from the school staff** who can provide specific support by regularly assisting the student with homework coordination and planning while also teaching these skills at the same time.

- Offer *specific* **homework help at home**, such as devising a work plan, starting individual tasks or problem solving if they get stuck. This avoids the impression of 'nagging'.

- Remember to apply the strategies from the 'Don't Miss A Thing!' and 'Getting Sorted' chapters to help with **concentration and organization**.

- Attending **homework clubs** at lunch time or after school can be really effective.

- **Consider motivators.** These can be 'natural' rewards such as fun activities after homework is complete, or more artificial (but effective) strategies such as earning tokens towards a specific reward.

- **Using a computer** can help with motivation, concentration and legibility of work. Ensure that all teachers are on board so that work can be submitted as typed work, even when that is not the format given (e.g. a print out attached to the worksheet).

- Considering the genuine difficulties experienced by young people with ADHD, it can be both highly effective and valid to **reduce the volume of homework demands**.

# Handwriting

The 'terrible handwriting' of young people with ADHD is a problem often quoted by teachers and parents alike. The impulsivity, restlessness, short attention span and processing difficulties associated with ADHD combine to have a significant impact on handwriting. Legibility is often affected by rushing, poor forward planning (e.g. layout) and minimal self-monitoring or checking. It is also important to recognize that young people with ADHD have a much greater chance of having coordination disorders. If there is evidence of difficulties in other motor skills, assessment and advice should be sought from an occupational therapist.

Regardless of the cause of the handwriting difficulties, there is one guaranteed way of making real and lasting improvements – **TYPING!** Using a computer helps on multiple levels, including benefits to the young person's attention (through the extra visual and movement stimulation), restlessness (as both hands are moving), organization (the spacing and margins are already set) and proof reading (such as visual prompts through spell check). It is also a life-long skill! Some tips for introducing and teaching typing include the following:

- Make an agreement with the young person in which a commitment to learning to type comes first. This is often easy to secure when the incentive is the opportunity to type rather than write! The aim is to make sure their typing is almost as fast as their writing (and remember that it is OK to be a bit slower if the product is actually legible!).

- Find fun ways of practising, including game-orientated typing programs, writing emails, copying lyrics from favourite songs and having speed typing competitions.

- Be creative in finding as many situations as possible in which typing can replace handwriting (e.g. using a laptop in class, typing all homework assignments).

- Remember to add strategies to help organize the loose sheets of paper once work is printed off (e.g. folders).

# Surviving Homework!

## BOOKS

- *Study Strategies Made Easy: A Practical Plan for School Success* by Leslie Davis and Sandi Sirotowitz, 1996, Speciality Press.

## TECHNOLOGY AND TOOLS

- Timers that give clear visual feedback on the passing of time (www.timetimer.com).

- Software programs that help to structure learning such as Inspiration (www.inspiration.com), which helps to plan, organize, research and present.

- Calendars and planning tools: these can be computer based (e.g. Microsoft Outlook, www.yourorganiser.com.au), utilize portable technology (e.g. linked to mobile phones/PDA) or paper diaries/organizers with additional structure (e.g. Tudor Organizer, Planner Pad).

## INTERNET SITES

- ADDitude; Living Well with ADD and Learning Disabilities:

  ○ www.additudemag.com/topic/adhd-learning-disabilities/homework-study-help

  ○ www.additudemag.com/adhd/article/1034.html

  ○ www.additudemag.com/adhd/article/2010.html

# CHAPTER 9

# The Future and Beyond

The aim of this final chapter is to help you pull together the detections, reflections and strategies you have discovered while working through the book, and move them into plans for the future and beyond. It will also give you and the young person a chance to reflect on your experiences, and to celebrate your hard work and successes.

At the end of each completed chapter you have identified those areas thought to be in need of further development and focused support (the 'Pulling It Together' pages). Now is the time to:

- prioritize these areas

- create specific goals and action plans

- put things into action

- make real and lasting changes!

Select only one or two skills to work on at a time to help focus your energy. Some people have found that, by sharing decisions, the young person's motivation and sense of ownership can be significantly increased (e.g. the young person chooses one skill and the adult the other). Try strategies for **at least four weeks** in order to ensure adequate practice to turn them into habits. Once successfully implemented, these strategies will become part of daily life, and you will be able to choose new goals to work towards. It is also important to recognize that priorities change over time, and you may need to revisit a section of the book at a later date.

From experience, we have learnt that in creating change and working towards goals, there are a few key elements to success. Some useful considerations are listed in the 'Top Tips' section of this chapter. However, the overarching principles for success include the following:

1. **Choosing goals that are valued** by those involved, so that everyone is motivated to achieve the outcome. Work towards having a clear but realistic 'picture' of what life will be like if the goal is achieved, and the multiple benefits it will have. Everyone should try to hold that image in mind!

2. Recognizing that achieving goals will **require additional resources and involve changes** for all. A real commitment of time and energy will be necessary for success, especially when people need to change their behaviour. If you can't commit adequate time, simply accept that you can't set the goals! Otherwise you will only be setting yourself and the young person up for failure. Conversely, if you are going to put in the effort and resources, you will want to ensure that there is the greatest chance of making a real difference, and this will often come down to effective goal setting (see below).

3. **Celebrating both effort and success** is vital in sustaining the process of growth and learning. For young people with ADHD and their support team, achieving goals takes extra effort, and additional motivators and rewards need to be added to provide the energy and motivation to continue. Remember that these celebrations are not just for the young person – the adults working with them also need to share the triumph!

4. Make working towards goals **part of daily lif**e and have everyone setting individual goals.

5. **Effective goal setting** is another significant element that demands thoughtful and careful planning. In recognition of this, the goal-setting sheets in this chapter are designed to help support a 'SMART' process. Good goal setting does not happen spontaneously, even for the most experienced of us. How many times have you set yourself a general goal such as 'getting fit'? How much better would it be to set yourself a 'SMARTer' goal such as 'Signing up to the gym and going twice each week for a month'? So what are SMART goals and how do you set them? The key ingredients to the SMART formula are as follows:

**S**pecific: Make goals specific so that they answer the six 'W' questions: who, what, where, when, which and why.

**M**easurable: Set definite criteria so progress can be measured – how much, how many, etc. This will ensure that everyone will know when the goal has been met.

**A**ttainable: Set smaller, more achievable goals, even if you have to set a number of smaller 'steps' before achieving a larger goal. Consider what is attainable in light of the time frame set (see below).

**R**ealistic: Use your knowledge of the young person's skills and the environment they are in to determine what is realistic. Be mindful that goals that include concepts such as 'always' and '100%' might never be achievable.

**T**imely: Set a definite time frame in which to achieve the goal. A shorter time frame will be more effective in keeping everyone on track and energized.

When it comes to setting goals based on the work you have completed in this book, there are many alternative formats that you can use. However, it is highly recommended that you keep these SMART principles in mind, and that you address the practical considerations outlined in the goal-setting worksheets we have included in this chapter. There is also an accompanying 'goal review' sheet included to help facilitate the second stage of the process.

Before you start your last series of 'Detect and Reflect', 'Give It A Go', 'Pulling It Together' and 'Top Tips', we would like to say CONGRATULATIONS, even if you have only flipped through this book. Understanding and empathy go a long way in making a real difference for young people with ADHD and their families. We hope you continue to enjoy the journey!

# The Best Bits (Young Person)

Take a few moments to think about the work you have completed so far in this book. Have a flick through all the sheets that you have done – that's a lot of work! In the shapes below draw or write some of the things you found the most fun, the most useful and the most interesting. It's important that the adult you have been working with does this as well, so there is a worksheet on the next page for them to do at the same time!

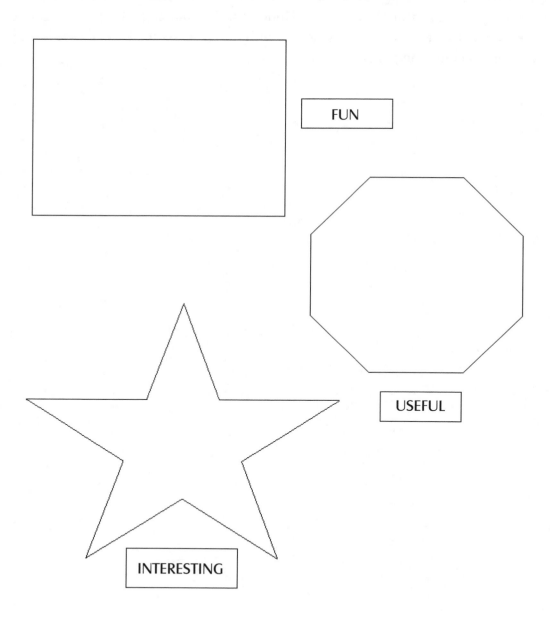

# The Best Bits (Adults)

Look back through your own folder and reflection sheets and think about all the work completed by yourself and the young person during the course of this book. Draw or write about what you found the most fun, the most useful and the most interesting in the shapes below. Compare your answers to each other's!

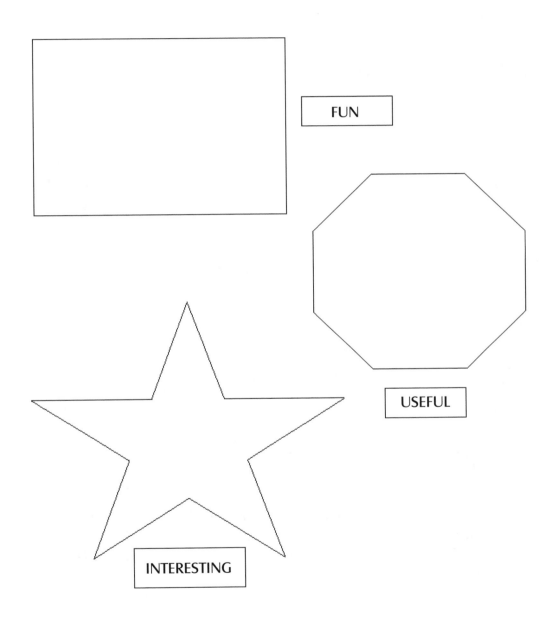

# Looking into a Crystal Ball

Imagine you have a crystal ball and can see two years into the future. What will your life be like? How will you be getting on in school? What activities or hobbies do you hope to be doing? How will you be managing your ADHD? What will be happening in your family? Draw some of your predictions in the crystal ball below or use key words and symbols if you would prefer.

# Identifying Goals

Now comes the fun part – putting ideas into action! Fill out the 'mind map' on the next page to help figure out which goals to work on, and in what order. Go through these steps:

1. Look back through all the 'Pulling It Together' sheets at the end of each chapter. For those that you have identified as an area to 'work on', write the name of the chapter into the circles in the mind map. Write each one in a different colour. If you need more circles draw them in or do your own mind map on a big sheet of paper.

2. From each circle, draw other lines and circles and write down important things from that particular chapter. These are the ideas that might help you figure out your goals, such as specific tasks you find difficult, and strategies you thought might work well.

3. Once this is done, choose the top three things that you would like to work on and highlight them. This could be a general skill area (e.g. making friends) or a particular strategy (e.g. setting up a homework station). Then ask the adult to highlight their top three in another colour.

4. Compare your top threes, and agree on one or two ideas to start with. These will become goals.

5. Read through the example goal sheets that Carly and James have filled out. It is hoped that they will help you to complete yours. You might need to have a meeting to set your goals, especially if they involve a few different people, but you can start the planning now.

6. Remember to keep the mind map because after you have achieved the first few goals, you can come back and pick out a few more!

# Identifying Goals: Mind Map

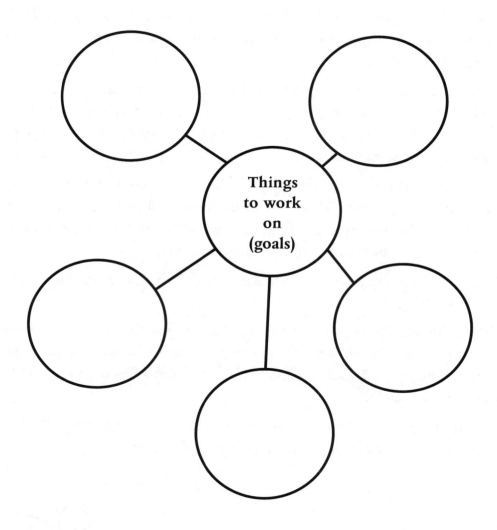

# Goal Setting

Carly and her Mum agreed a goal to work on – have a look at their ideas.

| GOAL SETTING FOR: Carly | Date: September |
|---|---|
| GENERAL AIM: | Complete more homework |
| SMART GOAL: (specific, measurable, attainable, realistic, timely) | To sit and concentrate on my Maths homework for 20 minutes when I use the helping strategies |
| WHAT STRATEGIES WILL BE USED: | Make a fidget<br>Organize my homework space<br>My teacher will write in my diary when Maths homework is due |
| WHO WILL DO WHAT: | Mum – buy balloons and flour for fidget<br>Carly – make fidget<br>Mum and Carly – tidy and organize desk in bedroom |
| HOW WILL WE KNOW IT IS WORKING AND WHO/HOW WILL YOU MEASURE THIS? | Maths homework will be started 100% of the time and finished 80% of the time<br>I won't get kept in at lunch to do my Maths homework |
| WHEN TO CHECK PROGRESS (min 4 weeks): | 6 weeks' time just before mid-term break – meeting with Mum and teacher |
| WHAT IS THE SMALL REWARD IF THE GOAL IS ACHIEVED? | Trip to the cinema at mid-term break – my choice of movie, popcorn and drink! |

James has agreed a goal to work on with his teacher and completed the worksheet below.

| GOAL SETTING FOR: James | Date: January |
| --- | --- |
| GENERAL AIM: | To stop getting so many detentions |
| SMART GOAL: (specific, measurable, attainable, realistic, timely) | To not get into fights with others during the lunch break by using the chill-out strategies |
| WHAT STRATEGIES WILL BE USED: | Think about my stress volcano and chill-out tips<br><br>Practise relaxation three times a week at home<br><br>Use my school chill-out space during lunch time |
| WHO WILL DO WHAT: | Dad – buy relaxation music CD<br><br>Head of Year – organize chill-out space<br><br>James – use these tactics and check in with Mrs Jones at the end of each lunch for a quick update |
| HOW WILL WE KNOW IT IS WORKING AND WHO/HOW WILL YOU MEASURE THIS? | I won't get any detentions for fighting at lunch time<br><br>The notes kept by James and Mrs Jones will show: no fights reported AND the chill-out space has been used |
| WHEN TO CHECK PROGRESS (min 4 weeks): | 1 month's time (meeting on Feb 20th) |
| WHAT IS THE SMALL REWARD IF THE GOAL IS ACHIEVED? | Invite friend over for a sleepover at the weekend<br><br>2 lunch-time passes to the computer rooms |

# Goal-Setting Sheet

| GOAL SETTING FOR: | Date: |
|---|---|
| GENERAL AIM: | |
| SMART GOAL:<br>(specific, measurable, attainable, realistic, timely) | |
| WHAT STRATEGIES WILL BE USED: | |
| WHO WILL DO WHAT: | |
| HOW WILL WE KNOW IT IS WORKING AND WHO/HOW WILL YOU MEASURE THIS? | |
| WHEN TO CHECK PROGRESS (min 4 weeks): | |
| WHAT IS THE SMALL REWARD IF THE GOAL IS ACHIEVED? | |

# Goal Review Sheet

| GOAL REVIEW FOR: | Date: |
|---|---|
| SMART GOAL: | |
| WAS THE GOAL MET? | |
| WAS THE PLAN FULLY PUT IN PLACE? | |
| WHICH STRATEGIES HELPED: | |
| WHICH STRATEGIES DIDN'T HELP: | |
| REWARD TO BE GIVEN: | |
| REFLECT ON THE ABOVE AND CHOOSE ONE OF THE FOLLOWING ACTIONS: | |
| 1. GOAL NOT MET: KEEP WORKING ON REVISED GOAL | Review the original goal-setting sheet and above – what changes are needed: |
| 2. GOAL MET: TRANSFER STRATEGIES INTO DAILY LIFE (CREATE A PLAN) | Agree systems for ongoing monitoring and rewards. Consider what level of external/adult support is required: |

# Congratulations!

The certificate on the next page is to congratulate you on all the hard work you have undertaken, so please fill it in and decorate it. You could also make another one for the adult who has helped you in working through this book! There are blank spaces so that all of the great traits that you displayed can be added, such as hard work, imagination, energy or thoughtfulness. Try photocopying the certificate onto coloured paper if you want to add some extra style!

You may also want to celebrate all your hard work and achievements in another way. Perhaps you could go out for an ice cream, have a special morning tea, or…

## Certificate

Certificate
of
Excellence !!

This award goes to:

_____

for :

# Survival Tips for Young People Living with ADHD

Some young adults with ADHD gave us the following tips to pass on to you:

- It's important that you can **talk to people** when you have questions, or feel confused, upset or uncertain about something to do with your ADHD. Try to always have at least one adult you can talk to about it – figure out who is a good listener and who seems to 'get' you.

- Try to **meet other people with ADHD** and share your ideas and experiences with them. Talk to them in person, in chat rooms, via email or send them letters.

- Be warned! **The internet** can be a great resource for finding out more information on ADHD. However, there are also things you might read that aren't accurate or are total rubbish! Discuss what you read with an adult and review the information together. Do your research and don't accept things just because they are on the net.

- It is important to **work as part of a team** with your family, your doctor and your school. Make sure you have your say, but also listen to other people's ideas and come up with solutions together. No person has all the answers.

- At school, work out which staff members are part of **your support network** (e.g. Form Tutor, Head of Year, Learning Support) and try to learn their names and where they are located. Go to them for help with sorting out problems rather than keeping things to yourself and getting upset or angry. They are there to help!

- **Surround yourself with great people** – people that you can rely on, who enjoy your company and who are good fun.

- Learn about all the good things that come with ADHD and that are a part of you. Remember to always **keep things in perspective** (i.e. balance the good and the not so good) and enjoy being an individual!

# Implementing Strategies and Working Towards Goals

It is important to recognize that creating change is hard work.

- **Take a problem-solving approach**: Remember that this is a learning process, and every young person and every setting will be different. Don't be worried about needing to change and improve on strategies – expect that, for things to really work well, adjustment will be necessary. Get ideas from multiple sources, and remember that the answer will often be linked to changing things AROUND the young person to enable them to have a fair shot at succeeding. Remember it takes at least four weeks to establish new habits, so don't give up too quickly.

- **Consider timing**: Give careful consideration to selecting the best time to implement things. What else is going on for you and the young person? Remember that high levels of stress can create barriers to learning. Also make sure you have time to follow through with things, otherwise you are setting yourself up for failure and unnecessary stress!

- **Work for success**: Keep expectations realistic. Start with very small goals that are easy to achieve so that these become early successes that will quickly build a positive momentum and a 'can do' attitude from all involved.

- **Grade tasks**: Sometimes you can continue with a specific goal, but gradually increase the challenge over time. For example, you can slowly increase expectations (e.g. expected concentration times) *or* gradually reduce the level of help offered (e.g. number of homework checks). Just don't fall into the trap of changing more than one thing at a time!

- **Communicate and share**: Make time to develop methods of sharing information from one teacher to another and between school and home. Take care to include any external professionals in this process. Also involve and empower the young person in this process (e.g. to attend meetings, carry 'update' cards with them to share with teachers).

# Survival Tips for Parents, Carers and Families

Looking after yourself and your family is an essential ingredient to supporting a young person with ADHD. A calm, stable, predictable home life provides an invaluable base from which the young person can explore and learn. By spending time looking after yourself, you ensure that you have the energy and ability to provide this safe haven for your child!

- Make regular times for fun family activities and schedule them in advance!

- Spend individual time with each child – even ten minutes can be really effective.

- Recognize and manage your own stress – you can even use tips from this book!

- Teach siblings and the wider family about ADHD (use the tip sheets and resources).

- Consider sharing information with others in the community (e.g. friends, other parents, coaches). This could be general information on ADHD or specifically about your child.

- Take on the role of 'Keeper of Information'. You will often be the expert on your child and can actively share this knowledge, and strive to *gradually* educate others about what life is like for your child and what approaches/strategies work well.

- Be willing to try new things and open to revisiting strategies that may have already been tried in the past.

- Keep good relationships with the school, even if this may be challenging at times.

- Find other parents who have children with ADHD or similar difficulties: share stories, problem solve, swap resources or just hang out over coffee or wine! Remember that the internet can be a convenient and effective means of connecting with others.

- Build positive stories and tell these all the time: positive stories about the family, about living with ADHD, about the young person, and about individuality.

- Seek help when you need it, either for yourself or your child. You might need to be prepared for long waiting lists and limited services. Try to find an inner strength that will help you to persevere in striving to access all the help you can.

# Survival Tips for Teachers and School Staff

1. **Understanding is the key:**

   - Provide training for all school staff on ADHD, including both teaching and ancillary staff.

   - Keep attuned and empathic – take stock every term and look beyond the behaviours to see the world from the young person's point of view (use some of the worksheets from the 'Welcome' chapter). Describe the young person's reality to another staff member to consolidate this.

   - Reflect on your own preferences and styles, and their 'fit' with the young person.

2. **Clear communication within the support team:**

   - Clear communication is essential for consistency, and shared learning and understanding.

   - Communicate with the family on a regular basis (e.g. diarized weekly or fortnightly meetings, communication books, identifying a mentor as a link person).

   - Develop a clear system for communication between the school staff. This takes time but is likely to be ONE OF THE MOST important factors in reducing problems at school, and could even be written into individual plans as a specific support strategy. Examples include:

     o regular meetings: updates at staff meetings, meetings with class teachers each term

     o information sheet on the wall of the staff room (similar to those used to flag allergies)

     o identified lead staff member who coordinates elements of the support plan and provides specific debriefing and problem solving to other staff

     o circulation of goal sheets and progress reports to staff

     o 'awards' to staff for implementing strategies (include details of their actions so as to provide concrete feedback and vicarious learning for others).

   - Seek help from specialists and get the most out of them by making requests specific (i.e. what do you want?). Providing detailed information is also crucial, including descriptions of behaviours, the level/nature of support needed and strategies attempted.

3.   **Support and empower the young person:**

- Develop a system of communication between the student and school staff, with the aim of creating a sense of support and empowerment for the young person. This could include laminated cards for the young person to hand to teachers as a reminder regarding special provisions (e.g. help with homework documentation); this is non-confrontational, avoids discussion in front of peers, supports staff and prevents problems with substitute teachers.

- Have a nominated teacher for the young person to 'check in' with on a regular basis. This teacher would help to facilitate perspective taking, problem solving and conflict resolution between the young person and peers and/or other teachers. This person doesn't need to be an expert in ADHD, but would ideally have an affinity with the young person and demonstrate aptitude in understanding and supporting them.

- Actively involve the young person with ADHD in planning, goal setting and reviews.

4.   **Create a positive culture:**

- Actively and regularly communicate the positives about the young person's participation and progress to family, school staff and the young person themselves.

- Build positive relationships between key school staff and the young person by spending small but powerful amounts of time doing fun or valued activities together, in particular things identified as preferences or specific interests by the student.

- Consider classroom withdrawal for targeted skill development, even in high school, as this support remains essential and one-to-one is the most effective means of delivery.

- Find ways for the young person to contribute to the school community; use their strengths, energy and interests.

# The Future and Beyond

## ADDITIONAL ADHD RESOURCES

- *Only a Mother Could Love Him: My Life With and Triumph Over ADD* by Ben Polis, 2004, Ballantine Books.
- *The Gift of ADHD: How to Transform Your Child's Problems into Strengths* by Lara Honos-Webb, 2005, New Harbinger Publications.
- *The Gift of ADHD Activity Book: 101 Ways to Turn Your Child's Problems into Strengths* by Lara Honos-Webb, 2008, New Harbinger Publications.
- *The ADHD Parenting Handbook: Practical Advice for Parents from Parents* by Colleen Roberts, 1994, Taylor Trade Publishing.

## BOOKS FOR SIBLINGS

- *My Brother's a World-Class Pain: A Sibling's Guide to ADHD-Hyperactivity* by Michael Gordon, 1992, GSI Publications.

## INTERNET SITES FOR THE FUTURE AS YOUNG ADULTS

- ADHD Centers: www.addcenters.com/Articles/teens%20transition.htm
- ADDvance: www.addvance.com/help/young_adults/index.html
- ADDISS (ADHD Information Services): www.addiss.co.uk
- ADDERS ADD/ADHD Online Support Group: www.adders.org
- Children and Adults with Attention Deficit/Hyperactivity Disorder: www.chadd.org

APPENDIX

# Pictures of Carly, James and Zac

**CARLY**

**JAMES**

203

**ZAC**